W9-BZH-178

In a society filled with so much anti-Christian rhetoric, there is no better book to equip Christians to think clearly, soundly, and inoffensively in the face of the devices employed today in opposition to the Christian faith.

— Norm Geisler
Author of *Encyclopedia of Christian Apologetics* and *When Skeptics Ask*

Greg Koukl is a master tactician. I know of no one who is more conscientious in his efforts to communicate effectively and winsomely his Christian faith. In this book Greg shares with us his tried and true methods, skills honed through continual practice and revision. Mastering his tactics will make you a more effective ambassador for Christ.

— William Lane Craig
Author of *Reasonable Faith — Christian Truth and Apologetics*

Just as a course on tactics is a requirement at all military academies, so too Greg Koukl's *Tactics: A Game Plan for Discussing Your Christian Convictions* should be required training for all Christians and churches. Koukl has made a worthwhile contribution to the literature on apologetics by teaching us *how* to say *what* we say. Witty and winsome, this resource is as fun to read as it is to put into practice.

— Hank Hanegraaff
Host of the "Bible Answer Man," author of *Christianity in Crisis: The 21st Century* and *The Complete Bible Answer Book, Collector's Edition*

C. S. Lewis once said, "Any fool can write *learned* language. The vernacular is the real test." In this book Greg Koukl passes Lewis's test with flying colors. There are many great arguments in favor of the Christian faith, but many of them are accessible only to professional apologists and philosophers. Koukl has developed a memorable and practical way to translate these arguments so that all Christians can become winsome and persuasive apologists in everyday conversations, no matter what their day jobs. This book should be required reading for every thoughtful Christian.

— Jay Wesley Richards
Coauthor of *The Privileged Planet*

If you enjoy apologetics, Greg's book *Tactics* is not only a required read, but simply a delightfully entertaining resource. In fact, just try and put it down! Especially for those who struggle with relevant ways to relate to non-Christians while presenting Christian truth, this volume provides many proven methods of natural, non-confrontational dialogue where the purpose is often to simply give an unbeliever something to think about, what Greg calls placing a stone in someone's shoe. Featuring remarkably simple techniques that are easily and fruitfully applied, this incredibly insightful book is one I highly recommend.

— Gary R. Habermas
Distinguished Research Professor, Liberty University
Author of *The Case for the Resurrection of Jesus*

With the advantage of a lifetime of experience, Greg Koukl has written what must be considered THE authoritative treatment of how to employ various strategies in conversations with unbelievers about the Christian faith. *Tactics* is not just another apologetics book. It is a sensitive, well-written, widely illustrated treatment of actual situations that often come up when believers share their faith. Koukl not only reminds us that it is not enough to know why you believe, but it is also crucial to know how to communicate those beliefs by adapting to various situations. And *Tactics* shows precisely how to do that.

— J. P. Moreland
Distinguished Professor of Philosophy, Talbot School of Theology,
and author of *Kingdom Triangle*

Greg Koukl has been using the methods offered in this book for many years with our Summit students and to great effect. His suggestions, illustrations, and witnessing approach work. This is a well-written, practical, and timely book.

— David Noebel
Founder and President, Summit Ministries

In this wise and compelling book, Greg Koukl — who has thought long and hard about not only what to say but how to say it — provides a game plan for equipping believers through an artful method of careful thinking and winsome conversation. If you struggle with how to talk about your faith and respond to questions and objections in a meaningful and effective way — and most of us do — there is no better book to buy, read, and put into practice. I could not recommend it more highly!

— Justin Taylor
"Between Two Worlds" blog.
Editor, *Suffering and the Sovereignty of God* and *The Supremacy of Christ in a Postmodern World*

Greg Koukl is a wise, seasoned, front-lines apologist. I am happy to recommend a book so full of practical insights and careful guidance for skillfully, winsomely defending the Christian faith.

— Paul Copan
Author of *True for You, But Not for Me* and *Will the Real Jesus Please Stand Up?*

Tactics is the book I've been waiting for! I love engaging non-Christians in conversation, but in the back of my mind I often think, "What if I get stuck and don't know what to do?" Greg helped me put that fear to rest and gave me practical tools to artfully maneuver in conversations. I enthusiastically recommend *Tactics*. It will revolutionize your conversations with non-Christians.

— Sean McDowell
Author of *Ethix*, coauthor of *Understanding Intelligent Design* and *Evidence for the Resurrection*

When I want someone who can help me train ambassadors for Christ, the first person I call is Greg Koukl. Now his proven ideas are in this book. I wish I had known these tactics twenty years ago. They are some of the best I've ever seen to help Christians be more effective ambassadors for Christ. Trust me — if you read Koukl's advice and learn his methods, your impact for Christ will skyrocket.

— Frank Turek
Author of *I Don't Have Enough Faith to Be an Atheist*

Greg Koukl is a master of the ideas that undergird the Gospel and one of the finest Christian communicators on the planet. He has spent many thousands of hours in front of the most difficult skeptics and their toughest questions and has developed very effective techniques to bring the truth to the surface of any conversation with love and grace.

I have learned so much over the years by studying his persuasive yet respectful approach to giving reasons for faith. This book presents his methods in a way that is engaging and accessible to every believer. I hope Christians in churches all over the country gather together to study this important book and learn to stand firm for the Gospel in these dark times.

— Craig J. Hazen, PhD
Founder and Director, Graduate Program in Christian Apologetics
Biola University

TACTICS

A GAME PLAN
FOR DISCUSSING YOUR
CHRISTIAN
CONVICTIONS

TACT🨙CS

Foreword by Lee Strobel

GREGORY KOUKL

ZONDERVAN®

ZONDERVAN

Tactics
Copyright © 2009 by Gregory Koukl

Requests for information should be addressed to:

Zondervan, 3900 *Sparks Dr. SE, Grand Rapids, Michigan 49546*

Library of Congress Cataloging-in-Publication Data

Koukl, Gregory, 1950–
    Tactics : a game plan for discussing your Christian convictions / Gregory Koukl.
        p. cm.
      Includes index.
      ISBN 978–0–310–28292–1 (softcover)
      1. Apologetics. 2. Evangelism. I. Title.
  BT1103.K68 2008
   239'—dc22   2008040292

All Scripture quotations, unless otherwise indicated, are taken from the *New American Standard Bible.* Copyright © 1960, 1962, 1963, 1968, 1971, 1972, 1973, 1975, 1977, 1995 by The Lockman Foundation. Used by permission.

Any Internet addresses (websites, blogs, etc.) and telephone numbers in this book are offered as a resource. They are not intended in any way to be or imply an endorsement by Zondervan, nor does Zondervan vouch for the content of these sites and numbers for the life of this book.

Interior design by Ben Fetterley

Printed in the United States of America

19 20 21 22 /DCI/ 35 34 33 32

To Annabeth Noelle
A light to my heart
By God's grace, a light to her generation

CONTENTS

FOREWORD

WHEN I hosted a national television program called *Faith Under Fire,* which featured short debates on spiritual topics, I decided to invite best-selling New Age author Deepak Chopra to be a guest. The topic would be the future of faith. To offer a different perspective, I asked my friend Greg Koukl to represent Christianity. The idea was to tape them as they interacted for about fifteen minutes via satellite, the typical format for a segment of the show.

That plan quickly went out the window.

Greg was simply so engaging and so effective in poking holes in Chopra's worldview that I had to keep the cameras running. Time after time, Greg was able to expose the faulty thinking underlying Chopra's amorphous theology and correct his inaccurate claims about Jesus and the Bible. Before I knew it, we had consumed the entire hour of the show. Chopra — who was accustomed to spouting his opinions unchallenged on television and radio — was left thoroughly defeated and deflated.

As soon as the taping was over, I turned to my producer. "That," I said, "was a textbook example of how to defend Christianity." For the only time in our show's tenure, we decided to devote an entire program to airing one debate.

Why was Greg so incredibly successful in that encounter? He wasn't belligerent or obnoxious. He didn't raise his voice or launch into a sermon. Instead, he used the kind of tactics that he describes in this book: winsomely using key questions and other techniques to guide the conversation and unveil the flawed assumptions and hidden contradictions in another person's positions.

That is what makes this book unique. There are plenty of resources that help Christians understand what they believe and why they believe it — and certainly those are vitally important. But it's equally crucial to know how to engage in a meaningful dialogue with a skeptic or a person from another religious viewpoint. This is the territory that this book covers with wit and wisdom, using examples from Greg's own life and insights gleaned from his years of fruitful ministry.

I had the privilege of having many of the country's top Christian apologists, or defenders of the faith, on my program — and Greg was consistently among the very best. When we needed someone to deal with some of the most difficult challenges facing Christianity for the film based on my book *The Case for Faith*, we again called on Greg — and once more he embodied what it means to be a prepared ambassador for Christ.

In fact, Greg is so good that Christians might say, "Well, he is really smart, uniquely gifted, and has a master's degree in this sort of thing. I could never do what he does." But they can — with a little help. One of Greg's driving passions has been to train ordinary Christians in how they can use easy-to-understand tactics to dissect another person's worldview and to advance the case for Christianity. He has been conducting seminars on this topic for quite a while — and I'm so thankful that he has now distilled his best material into this helpful and valuable volume.

We live in a day when militant atheism is on the march. Christianity is coming under attack, not just from best-selling books, skeptical college professors, and television documentaries, but increasingly from neighbors and co-workers. It has become a faux pas to claim that only one faith leads to God, that the New Testament is reliable, or that any tenet of neo-Darwinism might be open to question.

Each day the chances are increasing that you will find yourself in a conversation with someone who dismisses Christianity as a mythology-ridden anachronism. What will you do when they paint you into a rhetorical corner and belittle your beliefs? How will you persuasively present "the reason for the hope that you have" (1 Peter 3:15 TNIV)? How will you seize opportunities to get into potentially life-changing spiritual discussions with people you meet?

You've opened the right book. Let Greg be your mentor as you master new approaches to talking with others about Jesus. As Greg likes to say, "You don't need to hit home runs. You don't even need to get on base. Just getting up to bat — engaging others in friendly conversation — will do."

That means everyone can embark on this adventure. Take advantage of Greg's lifetime of study and experience by getting equipped now — so that God can use you "in season and out of season" (2 Timothy 4:2) to be his ambassador in a spiritually confused world.

—Lee Strobel,
Author of *The Case for the Real Jesus*

ACKNOWLEDGMENTS

I am thankful for the many people who have helped shape both the ideas in this book and the way I explain them to others. My wonderful team at Stand to Reason has challenged me, counseled me, and corrected me over the years and has had a major influence on the ideas in this book. My radio callers over nearly two decades have also helped sharpen my tactical skills.

Although the content of the manuscript is mine, I had a great deal of help with the wordsmithing. I am grateful for Nancy Ulrich and her wonderful "ear" for writing, for Amy Hall's thoughtful insights on structure, flow, and intellectual clarity, and for Susan Osborn of Christian Communicators, who gave the manuscript professional polish.

My agent, Mark Sweeney, smoothed out what is often a bumpy road to publication. He has also been a great sounding board and cheerleader whenever those talents were required.

I am especially grateful for STR's co-founder, the multi-talented, multi-tasking Melinda Penner, who does everything well. She makes my entire professional life possible and stabilizes a good deal of my personal life as well.

Finally and foremost, my gratitude to my most patient and durable wife, Steese Annie. Her cheerful heart does me good like a medicine, and her patience and gift of mercy are daily sources of grace to me.

Many of the ideas in this book first appeared in issues of *Solid Ground*, Stand to Reason's bimonthly newsletter available at www.str.org.

PART ONE

THE GAME PLAN

LET YOUR SPEECH ALWAYS BE WITH GRACE, SEASONED, AS IT WERE, WITH SALT, SO THAT YOU MAY KNOW HOW YOU SHOULD RESPOND TO EACH PERSON. (COLOSSIANS 4:6)

— Paul, the apostle

CHAPTER ONE

DIPLOMACY OR D-DAY?

Apologetics has a questionable reputation among non-aficionados. By definition, apologists *defend* the faith. They *defeat* false ideas. They *destroy* speculations raised up against the knowledge of God.

Those sound like fightin' words to many people: Circle the wagons. Hoist the drawbridge. Fix bayonets. Load weapons. Ready, aim, fire. It's not surprising, then, that believers and unbelievers alike associate apologetics with conflict. Defenders don't dialogue. They fight.

In addition to the image problem, apologists face another barrier. The truth is that effective persuasion in the twenty-first century requires more than having the right answers. It's too easy for postmoderns to ignore our facts, deny our claims, or simply yawn and walk away from the line we have drawn in the sand.

But sometimes they don't walk away. Instead, they stand and fight. We wade into battle only to face a barrage we can't handle. We have ignored one of the first rules of engagement: Never make a frontal assault on a superior force. Caught off balance, we tuck our tails between our legs and retreat — maybe for good.

I'd like to suggest a "more excellent way." Jesus said that when you find yourself as a sheep amidst wolves, be innocent, but shrewd (Matthew 10:16). Even though there is real warfare going on,[1] our engagements should look more like diplomacy than D-Day.

In this book I would like to teach you how to be diplomatic. I want to suggest a method I call the Ambassador Model. This approach trades more on friendly curiosity — a kind of relaxed diplomacy — than on confrontation.

Now I know that people have different emotional reactions to the idea of engaging others in controversial conversation. Some relish the encounter. Others are willing, but a bit nervous and uncertain. Still others try to avoid it entirely. What about you?

Wherever you find yourself on this scale, I want to help. If you're like a lot of people who pick up a book like this, you would like to make a difference for the kingdom, but you are not sure how to begin. I want to give you a game plan, a strategy to get involved in a way you never thought you could, yet with a tremendous margin of safety.

I am going to teach you how to navigate in conversations so that you stay in control — in a good way — even though your knowledge is limited. You may know nothing about answering challenges people raise against what you believe. You may even be a brand new Christian. It doesn't matter. I am going to introduce you to a handful of effective maneuvers — I call them tactics — that will help you stay in control.

Let me give you an example of what I mean.

THE WITCH IN WISCONSIN

Several years ago while on vacation at our family cabin in Wisconsin, my wife and I stopped at the one-hour photo in town. I noticed that the woman helping us had a large pentagram, a five-pointed star generally associated with the occult, dangling from her neck.

"Does that star have religious significance," I asked, pointing to the pendant, "or is it just jewelry?"

"Yes, it has religious significance," she answered. "The five points stand for earth, wind, fire, water, and spirit." Then she added, "I'm a pagan."

My wife, caught off guard by the woman's candor, couldn't suppress a laugh, then quickly apologized. "I'm sorry. I didn't mean to be rude. It's just that I have never heard anyone actually admit right out that they were pagan," she explained. She knew the term only as a pejorative used by her friends yelling at their kids: "Get in here, you bunch of pagans!"

"So you're Wiccan?" I continued.

She nodded. Yes, she was a witch. "It's an Earth religion," the woman explained, "like the Native Americans. We respect all life."

"If you respect all life," I said, "then I suppose you're pro-life on the abortion issue."

She shook her head. "No, actually I'm not. I'm pro-choice."

I was surprised. "Isn't that an unusual position for someone in Wicca to take, I mean, since you're committed to respecting all life?"

"You're right. It is odd," she admitted, then quickly qualified herself. "I know *I* could never do that. I mean, *I* could never kill a baby. I wouldn't do anything to hurt anyone else because it might come back on me."

Now this was a remarkable turn in the conversation for two reasons. First, notice the words she used to describe abortion. By her own admission, abortion was baby killing. The phrase wasn't a rhetorical flourish of mine; these were her own words. I did not have to persuade her that abortion took the life of an innocent human being. She already knew it.

She had just offered me a tremendous leg up in the discussion, and I was not going to turn it down. From then on I abandoned the word "abortion;" it would be "baby killing" instead.

Second, I thought it remarkable that her first reason for not hurting a defenseless child was self-interest — something bad might befall *her*. *Is that the best she could do?* I thought to myself. This comment itself was worth pursuing, but I ignored it and took a different tack.

"Well, maybe *you* wouldn't do anything to hurt a baby, but other people would," I countered. "Shouldn't we do something to stop *them* from killing babies?"

"I think women should have a choice," she countered without thinking.

Now, generally statements like "women should have a choice" are meaningless as they stand. Like the statement, "I have a right to take …," the claim requires an object. Choose … what? Take … what? No one has an open-ended right to choose. People only have the right to choose particular things. Whether anyone has a right to choose depends entirely on what choice they have in mind.

In this case, though, there was no ambiguity. The woman had already identified the choice: baby killing, to use her words. Even though she personally respected all life, including human life, this was not a belief she was comfortable "forcing" on others. Women should still have the choice to kill their own babies. That was her view.

Of course, she did not put it in so many words. This was her view *implicitly*.

When bizarre ideas like these are obviously implied, do not let them lurk in the shadows. Drag them into the light with a request for clarification. That is exactly what I did next.

"Do you mean women should have the choice to kill their own babies?"

"Well…." She thought for a moment. "I think all things should be taken into consideration on this question."

"Okay, tell me: What kind of considerations would make it all right to kill a baby?"

"Incest," she answered quickly.

"Hmm. Let me see if I understand. Let's just say I had a two-year-old child standing next to me who had been conceived as a result of incest. On your view, it seems, I should have the liberty to kill her. Is that right?"

This last question stopped her in her tracks. The notion was clearly absurd. It was also clear that she was deeply committed to her pro-choice views. She had no snappy response and had to pause for a moment and think. Finally, she said, "I'd have mixed feelings about that." It was the best she could do.

Of course, she meant this as a concession, but it was a desperately weak response ("Killing a two-year-old? Gee, you got me on that one. I'll have to think about it.")

"I hope so," was all I had the heart to say in response.

At this point I noticed a line of would-be customers forming behind me. Our conversation was now interfering with her work. It was time to abandon the pursuit. My wife and I finished our transaction, wished her well, and departed.

> Beware when rhetoric becomes a substitute for substance. You always know that a person has a weak position when he tries to accomplish with the clever use of words what argument alone cannot do.

I want you to notice a few things about this short encounter. First, there was no tension, no anxiety, and no awkwardness in the exchange. There was no confrontation, no defensiveness, and no discomfort. The discussion flowed easily and naturally.

Second, even so, I was completely in control of the conversation. I did this by using three important tactics, maneuvers I will explain in greater detail later in the book, to probe the young woman's ideas and begin to question her faulty thinking.

To start with, I asked seven specific questions. I used these questions to begin the conversation ("Does that star have religious significance or is it just jewelry?") and to gain information from her ("So you're Wiccan?"). I then used questions to expose what I thought were weaknesses in how she responded ("Do you mean women should have the choice to kill their own babies?").

I also gently challenged the inconsistent and contradictory nature of her views. On the one hand, she was a witch who respected all life. On the other hand, she was pro-choice on abortion, a procedure she characterized as "killing babies."

Finally, I tried to help her see the logical consequences of her beliefs. For her, incest was a legitimate reason to kill a baby. But when presented with a toddler conceived through incest, she balked. It had never occurred to her that, in her view, incest would be a legitimate reason to kill a two-year-old, and that gave her pause.

The third thing I want you to notice about our conversation is very important: The witch from Wisconsin was doing most of the work. The only real effort on my part was to pay attention to her responses and then steer the exchange in the direction I wanted it to go. That was not hard at all.

This is the value of using a tactical approach: staying in the driver's seat in conversations so you can productively direct the discussion, exposing faulty thinking and suggesting more fruitful alternatives along the way.

Regardless of your present capabilities, you can maneuver almost effortlessly in conversations just like I did if you learn the material in this book. I have taught these concepts to thousands of people like you and equipped them with the confidence and ability to have meaningful, productive conversations about spiritual things.

You *can* become an effective ambassador for Christ. It only requires that you pay attention to the guidelines in the chapters that follow and then begin to apply what you have learned.

TWENTY-FIRST-CENTURY AMBASSADORS

Representing Christ in the new millennium requires three basic skills. First, Christ's ambassadors need the basic *knowledge* necessary for the task. They must know the central message of God's kingdom and something about how to respond to the obstacles they'll encounter on their diplomatic mission.

However, it is not enough for followers of Jesus to have an accurately informed mind. Our knowledge must be tempered with the kind of *wisdom* that makes our message clear and persuasive. This requires the tools of a diplomat, not the weapons of a warrior, tactical skill rather than brute force.

Finally, our *character* can make or break our mission. Knowledge and wisdom are packaged in a person, so to speak. If that person does not embody the virtues of the kingdom he serves, he will undermine his message and handicap his efforts.

These three skills — knowledge, an accurately informed mind; wisdom, an artful method; and character, an attractive manner — play a part in every effective involvement with a nonbeliever. The second skill, tactical wisdom, is the main focus of this book.

Let's look at it another way. There is a difference between strategy and tactics. Strategy involves the big picture, the large-scale operation, one's positioning prior to engagement. We can apply this concept to our situation as Christians. As followers of Jesus, we have tremendous strategic superiority. We are well "positioned" on the field because of the content of our ideas. Our beliefs hold up well under serious scrutiny, especially considering the alternative views.

This strategic advantage includes two areas. The first, called "offensive apologetics," makes a positive case for Christianity by offering, for example, evidence for the existence of God, for the resurrection of Christ, or for the Christian faith through fulfilled prophecy. The second area, often called "defensive apologetics," answers challenges to Christianity like the attacks on the authority and reliability of the Bible, answering the problem of evil, or dealing with Darwinian macro-evolution, to name a few.[2]

Notice that in the way I am using the term, the "strategic" element focuses on content. Virtually every book ever written on defending the faith takes this approach. Faithful Christian authors have filled bookshelves with enough information to deal with every imaginable challenge to classical Christianity. Still, many Christians have an inferiority complex. Why? Maybe they have never been exposed to such excellent information. As a result, they are lacking the first skill of a good ambassador: knowledge.

But I think there is another reason. Something is still missing. A sharp lawyer needs more than facts to make his case in court. He needs to know how to use his knowledge well. In the same way, we need a plan to artfully manage the details of dialogues we have with others. This is where tactics come in.

TACTICS: THE MISSING PIECE OF THE PUZZLE

In World War II, the Allied forces had a strategic plan for gaining a foothold in the European continent. The Normandy invasion, code-named "Operation Overlord," involved a simultaneous attack on five beaches — Utah, Omaha, Gold, Juno, and Sword — on June 6, 1944, also known as D-Day.

No strategy, however brilliant, can win a war. The devil, as they say, is in the details. Individual soldiers must hit the beach and engage, deploying assets and destroying obstacles to gain an advantage, dodging bullets all the while.

Though we are following a diplomatic model and not a military one, the military metaphor is still helpful to distinguish strategy from tactics. Tactics, literally "the art of arranging," focus on the immediate situation at hand. They involve the orderly hands-on choreography of the particulars. Often a clever commander can gain the advantage over a larger force with superior strength or numbers through deft tactical maneuvering.

I think you can see the parallel for you as a Christian. You may have personal experience with how the gospel can change someone's life, but how do you design particular responses to particular people so you can begin to have an impact in specific situations?

Tactics can help because they offer techniques of maneuvering in what otherwise might be difficult conversations. They guide you in arranging your own resources in an artful way. They suggest approaches that anyone can use to be more persuasive, in part because they help you be more reasonable and thoughtful — instead of just emotional — about your convictions as a follower of Christ.

The tactical approach requires as much careful listening as thoughtful response. You have to be alert and pay attention so you can adapt to new information. This method resembles one-on-one basketball more than a game of chess. There are plans being played out, but there is constant motion and adjustment.

I have all kinds of odd names for these tactics to help you remember what they are and how they work — names like Columbo; Suicide; Taking the Roof Off; Rhodes Scholar; Just the Facts, Ma'am; and Steamroller. Some you initiate; others you use for self-protection.

In the pages that follow, you will encounter real-life examples and samples of dialogues where I use a tactical approach to address common objections, complaints, or assertions raised against the convictions you and I hold as followers of Jesus. But there is a danger I want you to be aware of, so I need to pause and make an important clarification.

Tactics are not manipulative tricks or slick ruses. They are not clever ploys to embarrass other people and force them to submit to your point of view. They are not meant to belittle or humiliate those who disagree so you can gain notches in your spiritual belt.

> It is not the Christian life to wound, embarrass, or play one-upmanship with colleagues, friends, or even opponents, but it's a common vice that anyone can easily fall into. — Hugh Hewitt[3]

I offer this warning for two reasons.

First, these tactics are powerful and can be abused. It's not difficult to make someone look silly when you master these techniques. A tactical approach can quickly show people how foolish some of their ideas are. Therefore, you must be careful not to use your tactics merely to assault others.[4]

Second, the illustrations in this book are abbreviated accounts of encounters I have actually had. In the retelling, I may appear more harsh or aggressive than I was in real life. I am not opposed to being assertive, direct, or challenging. However, I never intend to be abrasive or abusive.

My goal, rather, is to find clever ways to exploit someone's bad thinking for the purpose of guiding her to truth, yet remaining gracious and charitable at the same time. My aim is to manage, not manipulate; to control, not coerce; to finesse, not fight. I want the same for you.

If you are a little nervous about the prospect of talking to people outside the safety of your Christian circles, let me offer you a word of encouragement. I have been engaging challengers and critics in the marketplace of ideas for more than three decades. The people I talk with — atheists, cultists, skeptics, and secularists of every description — all oppose evangelical Christian views, sometimes vigorously and belligerently. Often they are very smart people.

To be candid, this concerned me at first. I wasn't sure how the ideas I'd learned in the safety of my study would fare against the smart guys in public with thousands of people watching or listening. What I discovered in the crucible, though, was that facts and sound reason are on our side. Most people, even the smart ones, don't give much thought to their opposition of Christianity. How do I know? I have listened to their objections.

You don't have to be frightened of the truth or of the adversaries. Take your time, do your homework, think through the issues. If Christianity is the truth, no matter how convincing the other side sounds at first, there will always be a fly in the ointment somewhere — a mistake in thinking, a wayward "fact," an unjustified conclusion. Keep looking for it. Sooner or later it will show up. Many times the right tactic will help you discover that flaw and show it for the error it is.

There is an art to this process, and learning any craft takes time and a little focused effort. It takes practice to turn a potentially volatile situation into an opportunity. If you learn the tactics in this book, though, I promise that you will get better at presenting the truth clearly — and sometimes even cleverly. I will guide you, step by step, through a game plan that will help you maneuver comfortably and graciously in conversations about your Christian convictions and values.

If you are an attentive student, in a very short time you will develop the art of maintaining appropriate control — what I call "staying in the driver's seat" — in discussions with others. You will learn how to navigate through the minefields to gain a footing or an advantage in conversations. In short, you will be learning to be a better diplomat — an ambassador for Jesus Christ.

WHAT WE LEARNED IN THIS CHAPTER

First, we learned the value of using the tactical approach when discussing Christianity. Tactics help you control the conversation by getting you into the driver's seat and keeping you there. Tactics also help you maneuver effectively in the midst of disagreement so that your engagements seem more like diplomacy than combat.

Second, we defined tactics and distinguished them from strategy. Strategy involves the big picture, which in our case means the content, information, and reasons why someone should believe Christianity is true. Tactics, on the other hand, involve the details of the engagement, the art of navigating through the conversation itself.

Third, we learned about the dangers of using tactics. Tactics are not tricks, slick ruses, or clever ploys that belittle or humiliate the other person. Instead, tactics are used to gain a footing, to maneuver, and to expose another person's bad thinking so you can guide him to truth.

Before we get into the details though, I would like to address a couple of possible reservations you may have.

CHAPTER TWO

RESERVATIONS

I have just made you a promise. I said that if you learn the tactics in this book, you will be able to comfortably engage in thoughtful conversations with others about your Christian convictions. At this point, though, you may have some reservations.

For one, trying to make your case with another person, even if done carefully, brings you dangerously close to having an argument. Some people think anything that looks like an argument should be avoided.

In one sense you'd be right. Squabbling, bickering, and quarreling are not very attractive, and they rarely produce anything good. With these types of caustic disputes, I have a general rule: If anyone in the discussion gets angry, you lose.

Here's what I mean. When you get angry, you look belligerent. You raise your voice, you scowl. You may even begin to break into the conversation before the other person is finished. Not only is this bad manners, but it begins to look like your ideas are not as good as you thought they were. Now you must resort to interruption and intimidation. You begin to replace persuasion with power. This is not a good strategy. It is never really convincing, even if you are successful in bullying the other person into silence.

What if you are able to keep your cool, but the person you're trying to persuade isn't? You lose in that case, too. People who are angry get defensive, and defensive people are not in a very good position to think about whether or not your ideas are good ones. Instead, they are too interested in defending their own turf.

> Always make it a goal to keep your conversations cordial. Sometimes that will not be possible. If a principled, charitable expression of your ideas makes someone mad, there's little you can do about it. Jesus' teaching made some people furious. Just make sure it's your **ideas** that offend and not **you**, that your **beliefs** cause the dispute and not your **behavior**.

It's good to avoid quarrels. Indeed, the apostle Paul tells us quite clearly that as the Lord's representatives, we must not be the kind of people who are looking for a fight. Rather, we're to be kind, patient, and gentle toward our opposition.[1]

There is another sense, though, in which arguments should not be avoided. I realize that for some people even a cordial defense of things like religious or moral views seems in bad taste. It sounds too judgmental and smacks of narrow-mindedness, even arrogance.

This is unfortunate. Let me try to explain why this second kind of arguing — contending in a principled way for something that really matters — is actually a good thing.

ARGUING IS A VIRTUE

Imagine living in a world in which you couldn't distinguish between truth and error. You would not be able to tell food from poison or friend from foe. You could not tell good from bad, right from wrong, healthy from unhealthy, or safe from unsafe. Such a world would be a dangerous place. You wouldn't survive long.

What protects us from the hazards of such a world? If you're a Christian, you might be tempted to say, "The Word of God protects us." Certainly, that's true, but the person who says that might be missing something else God has given us that is also vitally important. In fact, God's Word would be useless without it.

A different thing is necessary before we can accurately know what God is saying through his Word. Yes, the Bible is first in terms of *authority*, but something else is first in terms of the order of knowing: We cannot grasp the authoritative teaching of God's Word unless we use our minds properly. *Therefore the mind, not the Bible, is the very first line of defense God has given us against error.*

> The mind, not the Bible, is the very first line of defense God has given us against error.

For some of you this may be a controversial statement, so let's think about it for a moment. In order to understand the truth of the Bible accurately, our mental faculties must be intact and we must use them as God intended. We demonstrate this fact every time we disagree on an interpretation of a biblical passage and then give reasons why our view is better than another's. Simply put, we *argue* for our point of view, and if we argue well, we separate wheat from chaff, truth from error.

Jesus said, "You shall love the Lord your God with all your heart, and with all your soul, and with all your mind, and with all your strength" (Mark 12:30). Loving God with the mind is not a passive process. It is not enough to have sentimental religious thoughts. Rather, it involves coming to conclusions about God and his world based on revelation, observation, and careful reflection.

What is the tool we use in our observations of the world that helps us separate fact from fiction? That tool is reason, the ability to use our minds to sort through observations and draw accurate conclusions about reality. Rationality is one of the tools God has given us to acquire knowledge.

Generally, sorting things out is not a solitary enterprise. It's best done in the company of others who dispute our claims and offer competing ideas. In short, we argue. Sometimes we are silent partners, listening, not talking, but the process is going on in our minds just the same.

> The ability to argue well is vital for clear thinking. That's why arguments are good things. Arguing is a virtue because it helps us determine what is true and discard what is false.

This is not rationalism, a kind of idolatry of the mind that places man's thinking at the center of the universe. Rather, it's the proper use of one of the faculties God has given us to understand him and the world he has made.

FIGHT PHOBIC

If the notion of truth is central to Christianity, and the ability to argue is central to the task of knowing the truth, why do some Christians get upset when you try to find the truth through argument and disagreement? Two things come to mind that are especially applicable to those in a Christian setting, usually a church environment.

First, some fear division. When people are free to express strong differences of opinion, especially on theological issues, it threatens unity, they say. Consequently, the minute a disagreement surfaces, someone jumps in to shut down dissent in order to keep the peace. This is unfortunate.

True enough, Christians sometimes get distracted by useless disputes. Paul warns against wrangling about words and quarreling about foolish speculations (2 Timothy 2:14, 23). But he also commands us to be diligent workmen, handling the word of truth accurately (2 Timothy 2:15). And, because some disputes are vitally important, Paul solemnly charges us to reprove, rebuke, and exhort when necessary (2 Timothy 4:1 – 2). This cannot be done without some confrontation, but disagreement need not threaten genuine unity.

To be of one mind biblically doesn't mean that all have to share the same opinion. It means a warm fellowship based on communion with Christ in the midst of differences. It does not mean abandoning all attempts at refining our knowledge by enforcing an artificial unanimity. True maturity means learning how to disagree in an aggressive fashion, yet still maintaining a peaceful harmony in the church.

There's a second reason why Christians resist arguments. Some believers unfortunately take any opposition as hostility, especially if their own view is being challenged. In some circles it's virtually impossible to take exception to a cherished view or a respected teacher without being labeled malicious.

This is a dangerous attitude for the church because the minute one is labeled mean-spirited simply for raising an opposing view, debate is silenced. If we disqualify legitimate discussion, we compromise our ability to know the truth.

It is important not to deal with dissent in this way. Instead, we ought to learn how to argue in a principled way — fairly, reasonably, and graciously. We need to cultivate the ability to disagree with civility and not take opposition personally. We must also have the grace to allow our own views to be challenged with evidence, reasoning, and Scripture. Those who refuse to dispute have a poor chance of growing in their understanding of truth.

There is no reason to threaten our unity by frivolous debate. However, many debates are worthy of our best efforts. Paul told Timothy, "Retain the standard of sound words," and "Guard ... the treasure which has been entrusted to you" (2 Timothy 1:13 – 14). He told Titus to choose elders who could exhort in sound doctrine and to refute those who contradict, false teachers, he said, who must be silenced (Titus 1:9, 11). This kind of protection of truth is not a passive enterprise. It's active and energetic.

Arguments are good, and dispute is healthy. They clarify the truth and protect us from error and religious despotism. When the church discourages principled debates and a free flow of ideas, the result is shallow Christianity and a false sense of unity.

No one gets any practice learning how to field contrary views in a gracious and productive way. The oneness they share is contrived, not genuine. Worse, they lose the ability to separate the wheat from the chaff. Simply put, when arguments are few, error abounds.

DO ARGUMENTS WORK?

Now I want to address another question: Do arguments work? The simple answer is, "Yes, they do," but this needs explanation.

Some suspect that using reason isn't spiritual. "After all, you can't argue anyone into the kingdom," they say. "Only the Spirit can change a rebel's heart. Jesus was clear on this. No one can come to him unless the Father draws him (John 6:44). No intellectual argument could ever substitute for the act of sovereign grace necessary for sinners to come to their senses."

Of course, this last statement is entirely true as far as it goes. The problem is, it does not go far enough. There is more to the story. It doesn't follow that if God's Spirit plays a vital role, then reason and persuasion play none. In the apostle Paul's mind there was no conflict.

> And *according to Paul's custom*, he went to them, and for three Sabbaths *reasoned* with them from the Scriptures, explaining and *giving evidence* that the Christ had to suffer and rise again from the dead.... And *some of them were persuaded.* (Acts 17:2 – 4, italics added)

There are many more verses like this.[2] You might also be able to think of examples from your own life where taking a thoughtful approach with someone made a big difference in his response, maybe even a decisive difference.

Simply put, you *can* argue someone into the kingdom. It happens all the time. But when arguments are effective, they are not working in a vacuum.

When people say you can't argue anyone into the kingdom, they usually have an alternative approach in mind. They might be thinking that a genuine expression of love, kindness, and acceptance, coupled with a simple presentation of the gospel, is a more biblical approach.

If you are tempted to think this way, let me say something that may shock you: *You cannot love someone into the kingdom.* It can't be done. In fact, the simple gospel itself is not even adequate to do that job.

How do I know? Because many people who were treated with sacrificial love and kindness by Christians never surrendered to the Savior. Many who have heard a clear explanation of God's gift in Christ never put their trust in him.

In each case something was missing that, when present, always results in conversion. What's missing is that special work of the Father that Jesus referred to, drawing a lost soul into his arms (John 6:44). Of this work Jesus also said, "Of all that He has given Me I lose nothing, but raise it up on the last day" (John 6:39).

According to Jesus, then, two things are true. First, there is a particular work of God that is necessary to bring someone into the kingdom. Second, when present, this work cannot fail to accomplish its goal. Without the work of the Spirit, no argument — no matter how persuasive — will be effective. But neither will any act of love nor any simple presentation of the gospel. Add the Spirit, though, and the equation changes dramatically.

Here's the key principle: *Without God's work, nothing else works; but with God's work, many things work.* Under the influence of the Holy Spirit, love persuades. By the power of God, the gospel transforms. And with Jesus at work, arguments convince. God is happy to use each of these methods.

Why do you think God is just as pleased to use a good argument as a warm expression of love? Because both love and reason are consistent with God's own character. The same God who is the essence of love[3] also gave the invitation, "Come now, and let us reason together."[4] Therefore, both approaches honor him.

Understanding this truth makes our job as ambassadors much easier. We can be confident that every time we engage, we have an ally. Our job is to communicate the gospel as clearly, graciously, and persuasively as possible. God's job is to take it from there. We may plant the seeds or water the saplings, but God causes whatever increase comes from our efforts.[5]

> We are not in this alone. Yes, each of us has an important role to play, but all the pressure is on the Lord. Sharing the gospel is our task, but it's God's problem.

I like to call this principle "100% God and 100% man." I am wholly responsible for my side of the ledger, and God is entirely responsible for his. I focus on being faithful, but I trust God to be effective. Some will respond, and some will not. The results are his concern, not mine. This lifts a tremendous burden from my shoulders.

When I was a young Christian, the wife of my mentor gave me some solid advice from John 10. In this chapter Jesus uses a "figure of speech" (v. 6) to describe the work of the Holy Spirit drawing someone to Christ. "My sheep hear My voice," Jesus said. "I know them, and they follow Me; and I give eternal life to them, and they shall never perish" (John 10:27 – 28).

This has very practical application for evangelism because it helps explain something you might have encountered in conversations with others. Have you ever noticed that sometimes your comments seem to fall on deaf ears, yet at other times they seem profitable?

"When I share my faith," Kathy told me, "I pay attention to how the 'sheep' respond. Most will keep on eating grass. But once in a while you'll notice that some lift their heads. There is a moment of recognition as they 'hear' the Shepherd's 'voice.'"

Kathy understood that it was Jesus' job to change the heart. Since she was confident the Holy Spirit was going before her, she was simply looking for the people who were looking for her, so to speak. She was looking for those already hungry for the gospel, those whose hearts were already being softened by the Spirit. Those were the people she spent her time on. She left the rest alone.[6]

A MODEST GOAL

My confidence that God is responsible for the results helps me in another way. Since I know I play only one part in a larger process of bringing anyone to the Lord, I'm comfortable taking smaller steps toward that end.

It may surprise you to hear this, but I never set out to convert anyone. My aim is never to win someone to Christ. I have a more modest goal, one you might consider adopting as your own. *All I want to do is put a stone in someone's shoe.* I want to give him something worth thinking about, something he can't ignore because it continues to poke at him in a good way.

When a batter gets up to the plate, his goal isn't to win the ball game. That's an extended process that takes a team effort. He just wants a chance to get a hit. If he connects, he might get on base and into scoring position. Or he may drive another batter home, even if he never makes it to first. In the same way, I never try to hit the winning run. I just want to get up to bat. That's all.

In some circles there's pressure for Christian ambassadors to "close the sale," so to speak. Get right to the meat of the message. Give the simple gospel. If the person doesn't respond, you have still done your part. Shake the dust off your feet and move on. In my view, though, you don't have to get to the foot of the cross in every encounter. You don't have to try to close every deal. I have two reasons for this view.

First, not all Christians are good closers. Yes, some are effective at getting the decision. For those with that gift, harvesting takes little effort. Nothing fancy is required; the simple gospel does the trick. Yet I am convinced that most Christians — including me — are not harvesters. Instead, we are ordinary gardeners, tending the field so others can bring in the crop in due season. Some Christians, aware of their difficulty in harvesting, get discouraged and never get into the field at all. If this describes you, then you need to know it's okay to sow, even if you don't reap. In fact, there'd be no harvest at all without you. Ironically, I think harvesting comes easily for some because many ordinary gardeners preceded them — planting, watering, and weeding, cultivating healthy growth until the fruit was ripe.

Here's the second reason that I do not think it wise to make a beeline for the cross in every conversation: In most situations, the fruit is not ripe. The nonbeliever is simply not ready. She may have just begun to consider Christianity. Dropping a message on her that is, from her point of view, meaningless or simply unbelievable doesn't accomplish anything. In fact, it may be the worst thing you can do. She rejects a message she doesn't understand, and then she's harder to reach next time.

Think of your own journey to Christ. Chances are you didn't go from a standstill to total commitment. Instead, God dealt with you over a period of time. There was a period of reflection as you sorted out the details.

A few years back, I spoke to a Jewish attorney who didn't understand why he needed to believe in Jesus. In his case, I didn't try to build to a point of decision where I asked, "Do you want to receive Christ?" Instead, I put a stone in his shoe. I gave him two questions to think about. He needed to digest vital information before he'd be ready for a genuine commitment. If he ever made a decision to trust Jesus, I wanted it to be informed and thoughtful, a choice that lasted, not an emotional reaction made in the heat of the moment that he'd later abandon.

One spring I spoke in San Diego to an audience of four hundred students in a ballroom in the middle of the University of California campus there. Most were not Christians. I'd heard that the general attitude on campus was that Christians were stupid. That sounded like a good opener for my talk.

"I understand many of you think Christians are stupid," I said to the audience. "Well, many of them are," I admitted. "But many non-Christians are stupid, too, so I don't know how that helps you. What I want to do this evening is show you that *Christianity* is not stupid."

Then I shared with them my modest goal. "I'm not here to convert you tonight," I said. "Instead, I want to put a stone in your shoe." After that, I lectured on the failure of relativism. I wasn't there to close the sale. I just wanted to give them something to think about.

As it turned out, while taking questions from the audience afterward I was able to give more detail about the gospel, but only after I had laid the groundwork by making the message not only sensible to them, but reasonable. I took one step at a time.

> I encourage you to consider the strategy I use when God opens a door of opportunity for me. I pray quickly for wisdom, then ask myself this: What one thing can I say in this circumstance, what one question can I ask, what seed can I plant that will get the other person thinking? Then I simply try to put a stone in the person's shoe.

WHAT WE LEARNED IN THIS CHAPTER

I opened this chapter by addressing a handful of reservations you might have about developing your tactical skill as an ambassador. There is a difference between an argument and a fight. Unfriendly quarrels are not productive. If *anyone* in the conversation gets mad, then *you* lose. Arguments, on the other hand, are good things. Indeed, arguing is a virtue, because it advances clear thinking. If done well, it helps refine our understanding of truth.

When Christians avoid principled conflict on things that matter because of fear of disunity and division, they cripple the church in three ways. First, Scripture commands that we guard the truth within our ranks; where arguments are few, error abounds. Second, believers are denied the opportunity to learn how to argue among themselves in a fair, reasonable, and gracious way. Third, the outcome for fight-phobic churches is not genuine oneness, but a contrived unanimity, a shallow and artificial peace.

For those who are tempted to think that presenting arguments and evidence is not spiritual because only God can change a rebellious heart, I made two observations. First, without the work of God, nothing else will work — not arguments, not love, not even the simple gospel. Second, with the help of the Holy Spirit, God is pleased to use many things. Love and reason are especially appealing to him because both are consistent with his nature. The fact is, with God's help, arguments work all the time. Jesus used them, Peter used them, and Paul used them — all to great effect.

Understanding God's central role in the process removes a tremendous burden. We can focus on our job — being clear, gracious, and persuasive — and then leave the results to God (what I called "100% God and 100% man"). We're looking for those who are looking for us, in a sense — people whose hearts are already being touched by the Spirit. We can be alert for those sheep that hear Jesus' "voice" and lift their heads, without troubling those who are not yet ready.

Finally, I encouraged you to adopt the modest goal for your encounters that I have found so effective. Instead of trying to get to the cross in every encounter, just aim to put a stone in someone's shoe. Try to give the person something to think about. Be content to plant a seed that might later flourish under God's sovereign care.

CHAPTER THREE

GETTING IN THE DRIVER'S SEAT: THE COLUMBO TACTIC

LET'S start this chapter by putting you in a tough spot. I want you to imagine yourself in the following situations.

Scene 1: You're hosting a dinner party at your home for some of your close friends from church. The conversation ranges naturally over a number of interesting spiritual topics. Suddenly, to your surprise and embarrassment, your fifteen-year-old son announces with some belligerence that he doesn't believe in God anymore. "It's simply not rational," he says. "There is no proof." You had no idea he'd been moving in this direction. There's a stunned silence. What will you say?

Scene 2: It's the night of your weekly Bible study group. During the discussion of the Sunday sermon on the Great Commission, a newcomer remarks, "Who are we to say Christianity is better than any other religion? I think the essence of Jesus' teaching is love, the same as all religions. It's not our job to tell other people how to live or believe." The rest of the group fidgets awkwardly, but says nothing. How do you respond?

Scene 3: You're riding the university shuttle with a friend who notices a Bible in your backpack. "I've read the Bible before," he says. "It's got some interesting stories, but people take it too seriously. It was only written by men, after all, and men make mistakes." You try to recall the points your pastor made a few weeks earlier about the Bible's inspiration, but come up empty-handed. What do you say?

Scene 4: You're sitting at the car dealer, watching TV and waiting with other customers for your car to be serviced. A television news program highlights religious groups trying to influence important moral legislation. The person sitting next to you says, "Haven't these people ever heard of separation of church and state? Those Christians are always trying to force their views on everyone else. You can't legislate morality. Why don't they just leave the rest of us alone?" Other people are listening, and you don't want to create a scene, but you feel you must say something. What's your next move?

10-SECOND WINDOW

In each of these cases you have an opportunity, but there are obstacles. First, you must speak up quickly because the opportunity will not last long. You have only about 10 seconds before the door closes. Second, you're conflicted. You want to say something, but you are also concerned about being sensitive, keeping the peace, preserving friendships, and not looking extreme.

What if I told you there was an easy escape from the challenge that each situation above presents, a way to minimize the awkwardness and engage the other person productively and gracefully? What if you had a simple plan in place that would guide you in your next move? Would that give you the confidence to take a small step toward addressing challenges like these?

I have such a plan. My plan helps me know how to use that critical 10-second window to my best advantage. It acts as a guide to direct my next steps. When I consider each of the scenes above, a host of questions immediately come to mind. Later in the chapter I'll give you the back story to these questions. For the moment, think about how these responses begin to address the content of the person's remarks yet still draw him into an interactive conversation in a very intentional way.

Challenge 1: "It's not rational to believe in God. There is no proof."

What do you mean by "God," that is, what kind of God do you reject? What, specifically, is irrational about believing in God? Since you're concerned about proof for God's existence, what kind of evidence would you find acceptable?

Challenge 2: "Christianity is basically the same as all other religions. The main similarity is love. We shouldn't tell others how to live or believe."

How much have you studied other religions to compare the details and find a common theme? Why would the similarities be more important than the differences? I'm curious, what do you think Jesus' own attitude was on this issue? Did he think all religions were basically equal? Isn't telling people to love one another just another example of telling them how they should live and believe?

Challenge 3: "You can't take the Bible too seriously because it was only written by men, and men make mistakes."

Do you have any books in your library? Were those books written by humans? Do you find any truth in them? Is there a reason you think the Bible is less truthful or reliable than other books you own? Do people always make mistakes in what they write? Do you think that if God did exist, he would be capable of using humans to write down exactly what he wants? If not, why not?

Challenge 4: "It's wrong to force your views on other people. You can't legislate morality. Christians involved in politics violate the separation of church and state."

Do you vote? When you vote for someone, are you expecting your candidate to pass laws reflecting your own point of view? Wouldn't that essentially be forcing your views on others? How is that different from what you're troubled about here? Is it your view that only nonreligious people should be allowed to vote or participate in politics, or did I misunderstand you? Where, specifically, in the Constitution are religious people excluded from the political process? Can you give me an example of legislation that does not have a moral element to it?

I want you to notice several things about these responses. First, each is a question. My initial response in a situation like this is not to preach about my view or even disagree with theirs. Rather, I want to draw them out, to invite them to talk more about what they think. This takes a lot of pressure off me, because when I ask a question, the ball is back in their court. It also protects me from jumping to conclusions and unwittingly distorting their meaning.

> Asking questions enables you to escape the charge, "You're twisting my words." A question is a request for clarification specifically so that you **don't** twist their words. When I ask a clarification question, my goal is to **understand** a person's view (and its consequences), not to **distort** it.

Second, each of these questions is an invitation to thoughtful dialogue. Each is an encouragement to participate in conversation in a reflective way. Though my tone is relaxed and cordial, my questions are pointed enough to challenge the person to give some thought to what he's just said.

Third, these are not idle queries. I have a particular purpose for each question. With some, I'm simply gathering information ("Do you vote?"). Others, you might have noticed, are subtly leading; that is, the questions themselves suggest a problem with the other person's thinking ("Wouldn't that essentially be forcing your views on others?").

Each of the questions I have suggested above occur to me because I have a plan. I know that getting into conversations about spiritual matters is not easy, especially if someone's guard is up. It's not unusual to get tongue-tied, not knowing what to say. This is complicated by the fear of getting in over your head — or worse, of offending someone. We need some help.

Our first tactic is a handy solution to that problem. That's why I use it more than any other. It makes it easy for even the most timid to engage others in a meaningful way because it provides a step-by-step guide — a virtual game plan — to help ease into a conversation.

It might be called the "queen mother" of all tactics because it's so flexible and adaptable. It's easily combined with other moves you will learn later. It's the simplest tactic imaginable to stop a challenger in her tracks, turn the tables, and get her thinking, a virtually effortlessly way of putting you in the driver's seat of the conversation.

It's simply called "Columbo."

TAKE A TIP FROM LIEUTENANT COLUMBO

The Columbo tactic is named after Lieutenant Columbo, a brilliant TV detective with a clever way of catching a crook.

The inspector arrives on the scene in complete disarray, his hair an unkempt mop, his trench coat rumpled beyond repair, his cigar wedged tightly between stubby fingers. Columbo's pencil has gone missing again, so his notepad is useless until he bums a pen off a bystander.

To all appearances Columbo is bumbling, inept, and completely harmless. He couldn't think his way out of a wet paper bag, or so it seems. He's stupid, but he's stupid like a fox because the lieutenant has a simple plan that accounts for his remarkable success.

After poking around the crime scene, scratching his head, and muttering to himself, Lieutenant Columbo makes his trademark move. "I got a problem," he says as he rubs his furrowed brow.

"There's something about this thing that bothers me." He pauses a moment to ponder his predicament, then turns to his suspect. "You seem like a very intelligent person. Maybe you can clear it up for me. *Do you mind if I ask you a question?*"

The first query is innocent enough (if the lieutenant seems threatening, he'll scare off his prey), and for the moment he seems satisfied. As he turns on his heel to leave, though, he stops himself mid-stride. Something has just occurred to him. He turns back to the scene, raises his index finger, and says, "Just one more thing."

But "just one more" question leads to another. And another. Soon they come relentlessly, question after question, to the point of distraction and, ultimately, annoyance.

"I'm sorry," Columbo says to his beleaguered suspect. "I know I'm making a pest of myself. It's because I keep asking these questions. But I'll tell ya," he shrugs, "I can't help myself. It's a habit."

And this is a habit you want to get into.

The key to the Columbo tactic is to *go on the offensive in an inoffensive way by using carefully selected questions to productively advance the conversation*. Simply put, never make a statement, at least at first, when a question will do the job.

ADVANTAGES OF ASKING

There are dozens of fun ways to do this, and with a little practice it can become second nature. Hugh Hewitt, a nationally syndicated radio talk show host, is a master of this technique. In his wonderful little book *In, But Not Of*, a primer for Christians on thoughtful engagement with the culture, Hewitt advises asking at least a half-dozen questions in every conversation. It's a habit that offers tremendous advantages.

For one thing, sincere questions are friendly and flattering. They invite genial interaction on something the other person cares a lot about: her own ideas. "When you ask a question, you are displaying interest in the person asked," Hewitt writes. "Most people are not queried on many, if any, subjects. Their opinions are not solicited. To ask them is to be remembered fondly as a very interesting and gracious person in your own right."[1]

> Sometimes the little things have the greatest impact. Using simple leading questions is an almost effortless way to introduce spiritual topics to a conversation without seeming abrupt, rude, or pushy. Questions are engaging and interactive, probing yet amicable. Most important, they keep you in the driver's seat while someone else does all the work.

Second, you'll get an education. You'll leave a conversation knowing more than when you arrived. Sometimes that information will be just what you need to make a difference. When a young man asked me to recommend a book on Buddhism so he could witness to his Buddhist friend, I told him not to bother with the book. Instead, ask the Buddhist. Sit down over coffee and let him give the tutorial. It's a lot easier, he'd be learning the specifics of his friend's own convictions (instead of some academic version), and he'd be building a relationship at the same time.

Third, questions allow you to make progress on a point without being pushy. Since questions are largely neutral, or at least seem that way, they don't sound "preachy." When you ask a question, you aren't actually stating your own view. There's a further benefit here: If you are not pressing a point, you have nothing to prove and therefore nothing to defend. The pressure is off. You can relax and enjoy the conversation while you wait for an easy opening.

Once, during a dinner party at the home of a well-known comedian, I got into a spirited conversation with the actor's wife about animal rights. I had serious reservations about her ideas, but I didn't contradict her directly. Instead, I asked questions meant to expose some of the weaknesses I saw in her view.

Eventually, she began to challenge what she thought were my own views. I pointed out I'd never actually stated my beliefs.

I'd only been asking questions, so strictly speaking, there was nothing for me to defend. I didn't mind answering for my own views, but up to that point they had not come up. I was off the hook.

Finally, and most importantly, carefully placed questions put you in the driver's seat. "Being an asker allows you control of situations that statement-makers rarely achieve," Hewitt notes. "An alert questioner can judge when someone grows uneasy. But don't stop. Just change directions.... *Once you learn how to guide a conversation, you have also learned how to control it.*"[2]

It might have occurred to you that Jesus used this method frequently. When facing a hostile crowd, he often asked leading questions meant to challenge his audience or silence his detractors by exposing their foolishness: "Show Me a denarius. Whose likeness and inscription does it have?" (Luke 20:24); "Was the baptism of John from heaven or from men?" (Luke 20:4); "Which is easier, to say to the paralytic, 'Your sins are forgiven'; or to say, 'Arise, and take up your pallet and walk'?" (Mark 2:9).[3]

In none of these cases was Jesus speaking idly. He understood the power of a well-placed query. Whenever Jesus asked a question, he had a purpose. In the same way, the Columbo tactic is most powerful when you have a plan.

There are three basic ways to use Columbo. Each is launched by a different model question.[4] These three applications comprise the game plan I use to tame the most belligerent critic. Sometimes I simply want to *gather information*. Other times, I ask a question to *reverse the burden of proof*, that is, to encourage the other person to give the reasons for her own views. Finally, I use questions to *lead the conversation* in a specific direction.

"WHAT DO YOU MEAN BY THAT?"

When Lieutenant Columbo shows up at a crime scene, the first thing he does is gather facts. In the same way, sometimes you'll need more information before you can proceed in a conversation.

Your initial probe, then, will be open-ended: "What do you mean by that?" (or some variation).

This question provides a natural opening for conversation, and it puts no pressure on you. It's delivered in a mild, genuinely inquisitive fashion. It's a simple, virtually effortless way to use Columbo, and it has tremendous advantages.

First, this question immediately engages the nonbeliever (or the believer, if the difference of opinion is an in-house theological one) in an interactive way. This makes it an excellent conversation starter. When I noticed the jewelry worn by the witch in Wisconsin and asked, "Does that star have religious significance?" — a variation of "What do you mean by that?" — it led to a productive conversation.

> There are times when discretion is the better part of valor. For example, if your wife calls you an idiot, don't ask, "What do you mean by that?" She might oblige by clarifying.

Next, this question uncovers valuable information; it helps you know *what* a person thinks. There are two reasons this is important: You don't want to misunderstand him, and you don't want to misrepresent him.

Some questions or challenges are vague. It makes no sense to move forward if you're confused or unclear about what is being said. For example, the claim that "everything is relative" is wildly ambiguous. It should never pass without a request for clarification. Questions like, "What do you mean by 'relative'?" "Is *everything* relative?" and "Would that apply even to your own statement?" are all in order.

Other challenges are complex. They actually contain a number of specific issues jumbled together. For example, sometimes people claim that God is not necessary to explain morality; evolution can do the job. Since our survival depends on shared ethics, it's clear to them how natural selection could be involved in the process.

But this explanation hopelessly conflates two distinct notions. The first is Darwinian evolution which, by definition, can only explain morality in terms of *genetically determined physical traits* selected for survival (though one wonders how the rest of the animal kingdom seems to have endured very well without it). The second is the "evolution" of *intelligently designed civilization* from a primitive nuclear stage with each local tribe fending for itself, to a social contract stage enabling all to live together in safety and harmony. These are different issues. You may need to probe gently with questions to clear the confusion and then deal with each possibility on its own terms.

Second, if you don't understand a person's point, you may misrepresent it. This is a serious misstep, even when done by accident. Instead of fighting the real issue (your opponent's actual view), you set up a lifeless imitation (a "straw man") that you then easily knock down. If you're guilty of using the straw man fallacy, you may find you have given a brilliant refutation of a view the other person doesn't hold.

Sometimes the reason *you* are confused about another person's meaning is because *she* is confused, too. She objects to Christianity for reasons she hasn't thought through. The objection flourishes because no one has challenged the lack of clarity that led to the muddled thinking in the first place.

Don't be surprised, then, when your question "What do you mean by that?" is met with a blank stare. People don't know what they mean much of the time. Often they're merely repeating slogans. When you ask them to flesh out their concern, opinion, or point of view with more precision, they're struck mute. They are forced to think, maybe for the first time, about exactly what they do mean.

Be patient. Asking questions is the simplest way to clear up the confusion. It also gives you time to size up the situation and gather your thoughts.

Ironically, sometimes a bit more clarity is all that's needed to parry an objection. When someone says to me, "Reincarnation was originally part of Christian teaching, but was taken out of the Bible in the fourth century," I always ask them to explain how that works (a variation of our first Columbo question). The devil, as they say, is in the details of such a deception. How does someone remove select lines of text from tens of thousands of handwritten documents that had been circulating around the Mediterranean region for over three hundred years? This would be like trying to secretly remove a paragraph from all the copies of yesterday's *L.A. Times*. It can't be done.

> Be sure to pay attention to the response to your questions. If the meaning is still unclear, follow up with more queries. Say, "Let me see if I understand you on this." Then feed back the view to make sure you got it right.

Don't underestimate the power of the question "What do you mean by that?" Use it often. You can ask it in its many variations all day long. It will keep you engaged in productive, genial conversation while keeping the focus and the pressure on the other person, not on you.

10-SECOND WINDOW — REDUX

Earlier in this chapter I posed four different scenarios for you to consider. Then I offered a series of questions that I thought were appropriate responses to each one. My general goal was to use the Columbo tactic to get information, buy time, and steer things in a direction I thought might be productive. You may have wondered, though, why I chose the specific questions I did. Here was my thinking.

In "Scene 1," I noticed it was unclear what kind of God was being rejected. For some people, God is an old man with a beard sitting on a throne out in space somewhere. If that's the kind of God they *don't* believe in, then I agree with them. Some reject the notion of a personal God, but still believe in an impersonal god-force that animates the universe. Or it may turn out I'm simply dealing with good old-fashioned naturalistic, materialistic atheism. In any case, I need more information before I can continue.

Even when there seems to be little ambiguity in a remark, a clarification question, even a simple one, can break the tension of an awkward moment and buy you some time. It may even yield information you hadn't expected.

I hope you see the benefit of this minimalist approach, at least as a starting place. When you first encounter an atheist, you could launch into something like the kalam cosmological argument for God's existence — if you knew it, if you understood it, and if you remembered it — but that would be premature, wouldn't it? Why make things hard on yourself? A question serves you much better initially.

The demand for proof of God's existence is sometimes a trick. It may be a reasonable request for evidence, but often it is not. Unless you know in advance what kind of evidence would count (scientific? historical? philosophical arguments? revelation?) or what kind of "proof" would be satisfying (absolute proof? proof beyond a reasonable doubt? proof based on the preponderance of evidence?), you'll probably be wasting your time. It's too easy for an intellectually dishonest person to dismiss your efforts. "Not good enough," is all he needs to say.

The charge that belief in God is irrational is common, but completely without basis. I'm not going to let anyone who makes this assertion off easily. I want to know, specifically, how theism is at odds with good thinking. My Columbo question forces the person to spell out the problem instead of coasting on vague generalities.

Believing in leprechauns is irrational. Believing in God, by contrast, is like believing in atoms. The process is exactly the same. You follow the evidence of what you *can* see to conclude the existence of something you *cannot* see. The effect needs a cause adequate to explain it.

There is nothing irrational or unreasonable about the idea of a personal God creating the material universe. A Big Bang needs a "big Banger," it seems to me. A complex set of instructions (as in DNA) needs an author. A blueprint requires an engineer. A moral law needs a moral lawgiver. This is not a leap; it is a step of intelligent reflection. Therefore, the question "Specifically, what is irrational about believing in God?" is completely in order.

"Scene 2" presents another common challenge: religious pluralism. My questions were meant to capitalize on a number of weaknesses.

First, the comments show a naïve understanding of other religions (they actually vary wildly in fundamental beliefs). Second, pluralism presumes that the similarities between faiths are more important than the differences. Are aspirin and arsenic basically the same because they both come in tablet form? For some things, the differences are critical. Religion is one of them.

It's also clear that Jesus was not a pluralist.[5] As an observant Jew, he held to the Ten Commandments. Foremost among them was the first: The Lord is God and we owe fidelity to him alone. All other religions are distortions and deceptions. The early followers of Christ were first called "Christians" in Antioch by *others* (Acts 11:26). Their name for *themselves* was simply "the Way" (Acts 9:2; 19:9, 23; 22:4, 24:14, 22).

Did you notice, by the way, that this "Scene 2" person's minimal theology ("The essence of Jesus' teaching is love, not telling other people how to live or believe") does not allow him to escape his own charge? He has his own theological convictions — love, not judgment — that he thinks should govern how other people think and believe. This, of course, is a judgment itself. That's why I asked, "Isn't telling people to love one another just another example of telling them how they should live and believe?"

In "Scene 3," the key word is "only," as in "the Bible was *only* written by men." Notice that the statement itself presumes what it's attempting to prove, that the Bible is a purely human document. Since this is the very question at issue, the attempt is circular.

But there's a more fundamental problem. Even without God's help, fallible human beings sometimes get it right. Our libraries are filled with books written by mere mortals who seem completely capable of accuracy, insight, and wisdom. If this is true of so many others, why not of Paul, Peter, John, or Jesus?

I understand that this is not a slam-dunk argument for inspiration. It is not meant to be. Remember, my goal is modest. I want to put a stone in the person's shoe. I want to get him thinking. I want him to consider listening to Jesus first before dismissing him. If I can simply open that door, I have accomplished something important. Here's why.

Most people who believe in the authority of the Bible did not come to this conviction through argument, but through encounter.[6] For example, when soldiers were sent to arrest Jesus early in his ministry, they returned empty-handed. Why had they disobeyed orders? Because they had *listened*. "Never did a man speak the way this man speaks," they said (John 7:46). Jesus didn't start his discourse with reasons why people should believe his words. Instead, he simply spoke the truth, and it immediately resonated with many in the crowd.

I came to believe the Bible was God's Word in the same way I suspect you did. I encountered the truth firsthand and was moved by it. If you want skeptics to believe in the Bible, don't get into a tug-of-war with them about inspiration. Instead, invite them to listen — to engage Jesus' words firsthand — then let the Spirit do the heavy lifting for you.

So when someone says the Bible was "only written by men," I ask questions to encourage him or her to treat Jesus like any other teacher. I want that person to listen to the words of Jesus first, then draw conclusions. In my travel bag, I keep copies of John's Gospel, and I offer one as a gift, suggesting, "It might be best to let Jesus speak for himself." Once my new friend has read a bit, any further reasons I give for biblical authority will have the soil needed to take root.

It's easy to see the problem with the first challenge in "Scene 4" ("It's wrong to force your views on other people"). Those who are sensitive about "forcing" viewpoints have no business participating in a legislative process that does just that, ergo the question, "Do you vote?"

As to legislating morality, Aristotle famously observed that all law rests upon a necessary foundation of morality. If the government's exercise of power is not in the service of the common good, then its actions are illicit. Simply put, morality is the only thing you *can* legislate.

> Sometimes this first Columbo question is directed at a specific statement or topic of discussion. Other times, the question can be more open-ended. As the dialogue continues, gently guide the conversation into a more spiritually productive direction with additional questions.

WHAT WE LEARNED IN THIS CHAPTER

We started the chapter with a challenge. I gave you the opportunity to consider what you would say in the 10-second window of time available to respond to some standard challenges you might encounter as a Christian ambassador. Then I began to outline a simple plan as a guide to direct your steps. This plan is called "Columbo."

The Columbo tactic is a disarming way to go on the offensive with carefully selected questions that productively advance the conversation. This approach has many advantages. Questions can be excellent *conversation starters*. They are *interactive* by nature, inviting others to participate in dialogue. They are *neutral*, protecting you from getting "preachy," helping you make headway without stating your case. Questions *buy valuable time*. Finally, they are essential to keeping you in *control* of the conversation.

Next we learned there is a specific purpose for the questions we ask. The first purpose of Columbo is to gain information. The question, "What do you mean by that?" (or some variation) accomplishes that end. It clarifies the person's meaning so that you don't misunderstand or misrepresent it. It also immediately puts you in control of the conversation.

This question does something else that's very important. It forces the other person to think more carefully about precisely what he does mean when he tosses out a challenge. Instead of settling for statements that are ambiguous or vague, we ask him to spell out his objection clearly. We then looked in some detail at four very specific challenges to see how this works.

The question "What do you mean by that?" is your first step to managing conversations. Use it often. In the next chapter we will add another step to our game plan, the second use of the Columbo tactic.

CHAPTER FOUR

COLUMBO STEP TWO: THE BURDEN OF PROOF

SOME people think Christians are the only ones who need to answer for their beliefs. Of course, we should be able to give reasons for what we think is true. But we are not the only ones; others should be able to do this, too.

It's not unusual, though, for people to forget that they have this responsibility. At times they seem to think that all they have to do is tell a really good story and they have done their job. You might call this a "bedtime story." They conjure up a tale meant to put your view or your argument to rest. But this will not do. They might just as well have started with "Once upon a time." When you understand this, your job as an ambassador will be much easier.

If you have watched any reruns of *I Love Lucy* (or if you are old enough, like me, to remember the first runs), you might recall Ricky Ricardo saying, "Lucy, you've got a lot of 'splainin' to do." Ricky's statement applies here, too. People on the other side of your opinion have a lot of "splainin" to do themselves, and it's your job to get them to do it.

Many challenges to Christianity thrive on vague generalities and forceful but vacuous slogans. How do we help others to be more explicit about the reasons for their views? How do we keep them intellectually honest? The second step of Columbo will help. I call it "reversing the burden of proof."

The burden of proof is the responsibility someone has to defend or give evidence for his view. Generally, the rule can be summed up this way: Whoever makes the claim bears the burden. The key here is not to allow yourself to be thrust into a defensive position when the other person is making the claim. It's not your duty to prove him wrong. It's his duty to prove his view. Let me give you an example of what I mean.

COSMIC CONFUSION

Once I was a guest on the top-rated secular radio station in Los Angeles. The topic was intelligent design over evolution. When a caller used the Big Bang to argue against a Creator, I pointed out that the Big Bang worked in my favor. Then I used my "a Big Bang needs a Big Banger" line. This always gets a laugh, but it is also a clever way to make a good point.

The caller disagreed: The Big Bang doesn't need God. "You could start with a base of nothing," he explained, "and *you could say that* there was nothing but an infinite, continuous moment, until one tiny, little, insignificant thing happened: a point happened in the nothingness."

Now I know what you are probably thinking. How do you start with nothing and then end up with something? How do you get a point in the nothingness? Hardly a "tiny, little, insignificant thing." If your bank account has no balance, there's no sense checking the statement every month to see if you've earned interest.[1] The thought, apparently, did not occur to the caller, however. Facts, as C. S. Lewis once noted, can be very inconvenient things.

"This requires no intelligence," he continued, "so no intelligent God had to intervene. All we need is a tiny imperfection in the perfect nothingness that expanded and became increasingly complex, and soon you have galaxies and planets."

"You're right about one thing," I responded. "When you start with 'You could say that ...' you can spin any yarn you want. But then comes the hard part: giving reasons why anyone should take your science-fiction story seriously. It's not *my* job to *disprove* your something-from-nothing fairy tale. It's *your* job to *prove* it. You haven't done that. You haven't even tried."

You might have heard the phrase "throw down the gauntlet" and wondered what it meant. A "gauntlet" was an armored glove worn by medieval knights. When a knight threw his gauntlet into the arena, it was a challenge to another knight to "take up the gauntlet" and square off for a fight.

The caller on this radio show had thrown down his "gauntlet" and then expected to walk off with the prize without a struggle. This happens all the time. But I wasn't going to let him off that easily, and neither should you. For too long we have let others contrive fanciful challenges and then sit back and watch us squirm. Those days are over. No more free rides. If they tell the story, let them defend it. They need to give an argument.

A HOUSE WITHOUT WALLS

An argument is a specific kind of thing. Think of an argument like a simple house, a roof supported by walls. The roof is the conclusion, and the walls are the supporting ideas. By testing the walls, we can see if they are strong enough to keep the roof from tumbling down. If the walls are solid, the conclusion rests securely on its supporting structure. If the walls collapse, the roof goes flat and the argument is defeated.

Some arguments are not really arguments at all. Many people try to build their roof right on the ground. Instead of erecting solid walls (the supporting ideas that hold the conclusion up), they simply make assertions and then pound the podium — or verbally pound you.

An argument is different from an assertion, though. An assertion simply states a point. An argument gives supporting reasons why the point should be taken seriously. The reasons, then, become the topic of mutual discussion or analysis. But if there are no reasons, there's little to discuss. Opinions by themselves are not proof. Intelligent belief requires reasons.

Roofs are useless when they are on the ground. No one can live in a house without walls. In the same way, an assertion without evidence is not very useful.

I frequently get calls on my radio show from people who think they are giving me an argument when all they are doing is forcefully stating a view. This may sound compelling at first, and their story may even seem plausible. But there is a difference between giving an explanation and giving evidence the explanation is actually true. Your job is to recognize when the roof is lying flat on the ground and simply point it out.

> Don't let someone flatten you by dropping a roof on your head. Make him build walls underneath his roof. Ask him for reasons or facts to support his conclusions.

"HOW DID YOU COME TO THAT CONCLUSION?"

Our second Columbo question, "Now, how did you come to that conclusion?" is designed to enforce the burden-of-proof rule. Remember, this is a model question. You might also ask, "Why do you say that?," "What are your reasons for holding that view?," "What makes you think that's the right way to see it?," or "I'm curious. Why would that idea seem compelling to you?"[2]

The first Columbo question helps you know *what* another person thinks. This second question helps you know *why* he thinks the way he does. It charitably assumes he has actually come to a conclusion — that he has reasons for his view and not merely strong feelings about it. It will give him a chance to express his rationale, if he has any. It will also give you more material to work with in addressing his objections.

You may be surprised to know that most critics are not prepared to defend *their* faith. So don't be startled if you get a blank stare. Many people have never thought through their views and don't know why they hold them.

Caught off guard, some will quip, "I don't have any reasons — I just believe it." This is a remarkable admission. It is also a very foolish thing to say. In this situation I always ask, "Why would you believe something when you have no reason to think it's true?" Notice that this is just a variation of our second Columbo question. Do you see how simple that is?

The question "Now, how did you come to that conclusion?" accomplishes something vitally important. It forces persons you are in conversation with to give an account for their own beliefs. Christians should not be the only ones who have to defend their views. Reject the impulse to counter every assertion someone manufactures. Don't try to refute every tale spun out of thin air. Instead, steer the burden of proof back on the other person's shoulders. Make them give you *reasons*, not just a point of view. It's not your job to defeat their claim. It's their job to defend it.

This step of the Columbo tactic trades on a very important notion: *An alternate explanation is not a refutation.* Here's what I mean. It's not uncommon for someone to say, "Oh, I can explain that," then conjure up a story that supports her view. But I hope you see that giving an explanation is not the same as giving an argument — or refuting someone else's argument. She has to do more.

Oxford biologist Richard Dawkins wrote a landmark work entitled *The Blind Watchmaker*. Notice the way he explains how flight might have evolved:

> How did wings get their start? Many animals leap from bough to bough, and sometimes fall to the ground. Especially in a small animal, the whole body surface catches the air and assists the leap, or breaks the fall, by acting as a crude aerofoil. Any tendency to increase the ratio of surface area to weight would help, for example, flaps of skin growing out in the angles of joints. From here, there is a continuous series of gradations to gliding wings, and hence to flapping wings.[3]

Of course, this explanation may be a good one if you are a Darwinist. Stories like this are meant to parry objections, and this particular one has a good track record. This is partly because it sounds plausible enough at first (if it didn't, it wouldn't be appealing), and partly because it shields the Darwinian paradigm from a certain kind of criticism.

Don't misunderstand me. Starting with a hypothetical explanation is not in itself the difficulty. Science, forensics, and normal day-to-day problem solving trade on this ability all the time. Imagining what might have taken place may be a legitimate *first* step. It is not the last one, though, because a story doesn't settle anything. More is required.

In the case of flight, Dawkins's breezy account obscures two obstacles. First is the need for a massive infusion of new genetic information — at just the right time and in just the right balance — to accomplish the prodigious structural changes needed for flight. Second is the mechanical, sensory, psychomotor alterations required for the kind of flight that evolution could take advantage of. In order to overcome these serious hurdles, Dawkins needs to show the detailed and precise evolutionary pathways in specific cases of flight (birds, for example). This he does not do.

Explanations like Dawkins's are common in Darwinian circles. They are known derisively as "just so stories" after Rudyard Kipling's book of that title, a children's book with chapters like "How the Leopard Got His Spots" and "How the Camel Got His Hump." But stories like these pop up outside of Darwinism, too. Make sure you are not lulled to sleep by them. There are three questions you should always ask whenever someone offers an alternate explanation: Is it possible? Is it plausible? Is it probable?

First, is it *possible*? Some options seem completely unworkable on closer examination. In chapter 3, I questioned the view that the teaching of reincarnation was secretly removed from the Bible sometime during the fourth century. Such editing would require deleting selected lines of text from tens of thousands of handwritten New Testament documents that had been circulating around the Roman Empire for three hundred years. This could not happen. The "point in the nothingness" explanation for the Big Bang fails for the same reason. It's not possible to get something from nothing.

Second, is it *plausible*? Is it reasonable to think something like this *might* have taken place, given the evidence? Many things are possible that are not plausible. It is *possible*, for example, that I would have liver for dinner tonight. Nothing, in principle, prevents that from happening. It is not *plausible,* however. The reason is simple — I hate liver. Therefore, no one would ever be justified in thinking liver would be on my dinner plate at suppertime.

Some people claim that the miracles recorded in the Gospels were an invention of the early church to help consolidate its power over the people. Is there any evidence that this is what actually took place? It may be theoretically possible, but is it plausible? Does it fit the facts?

Third, is it *probable*? Is it the best explanation, considering the competing options? The person you're talking with must be able to show why his view is more likely than the one you are offering. For this he needs reasons. Why is his explanation a better one than yours?

When it comes to weighty matters, we want to make smart choices. Why go with a long shot, especially when so much might be riding on a decision? Wisdom, careful thinking, and ordinary common sense always side with the odds-on favorite. It may seem plausible to some that monkeys banging on typewriters long enough could eventually pound out the works of Shakespeare. That doesn't mean we're justified in thinking a baboon wrote *Hamlet.* I'm still convinced Shakespeare did that.

This is why your second Columbo question, "How did you come to that conclusion?" is so powerful. It helps you handle outlandish speculations and bizarre alternate explanations by placing the burden of proof where it belongs, on the shoulders of the one making the claim.

> Reversing the burden of proof is not a trick to avoid defending our own ideas. When we give opinions, we have to answer for them just like anyone else. We have a responsibility, but so do they — that's my point.

If you find yourself stymied in a discussion, you may be looking for an argument that isn't there. It may be a bedtime story or an unsubstantiated assertion. Simply ask yourself, "Did he give me an argument, or did he just give me an opinion?" If the latter, then say, "Well, that's an interesting point of view, but what's your argument? How did you come to that conclusion? Why should I take your point seriously? Please take a moment and give me some of your reasons." When he answers you, be alert to the differences between what is *possible*, what is *plausible*, and what is *likely*, given the evidence.

There are only a few exceptions to the burden-of-proof rule, and they are usually obvious. We are not obligated, for example, to prove our own existence, to defend self-evident truths (e.g., denial of square circles), or to justify the basic reliability of our senses. The way things appear to be are probably the way they actually are unless we have good reason to believe otherwise.[4] This principle keeps us alive every day. It doesn't need defending.

This second use of Columbo is not a trick to avoid shouldering the burden of proof. Rather, it's meant to ward off extreme and unfounded doubt. Just because it is *possible* to be mistaken about something that seems obvious doesn't mean it's *reasonable* to think we are. This is the skeptic's error. Do not be taken in by it.

THE PROFESSOR'S PLOY

The Columbo tactic is a good one to use in the classroom, but there is a pitfall. I call it the "professor's ploy." Some professors are fond of taking potshots at Christianity with remarks like "The Bible is just a bunch of fables," even if the topic of the class has nothing to do with religious issues. Well-meaning believers sometimes take up the challenge and attempt a head-to-head duel with the professor.

Don't make this mistake. It's right-hearted, but wrong-headed. This approach rarely works because it violates a fundamental rule of engagement: Never make a frontal assault on a superior force in an entrenched position. An unwritten law of nature seems to govern exchanges like these: The man with the microphone wins. The professor always has the strategic advantage, and he knows it. It's foolish to get into a power struggle when you are out-gunned.

There's a better way. Don't disengage. Instead, use your tactics. Raise your hand and ask a question. For starters, you might ask, "Professor, can you give us a little more detail on what you mean? What kind of fable are you talking about? Do you think nothing in the biblical documents has any historical value? Is everything in the book a fanciful invention of some sort? What's your opinion?" Notice that these are all creative variations of our first Columbo question ("What do you mean by that?").

Let the professor explain himself. As a good student, listen carefully to his response. Take notes. Ask further clarification questions if necessary. If he falters in any way, the other students will notice. If he has trouble making his ideas clear, it will become obvious that he has not thought carefully about his ideas.

When you are satisfied that you have a clear take on his view, raise your hand again and ask him how he came to his conclusions. Ask him to explain the line of evidence that convinced him not to take the Bible seriously. Make the teacher, the one making the claim, shoulder the burden of proof for his own assertions. This allows you to stay engaged while deftly sidestepping the power struggle.

Now here's the pitfall I warned you about, the distractive "ploy" intended to derail your efforts. The professor may sense your maneuver and try to turn the tables. He might say something like, "Oh, you must be one of those Fundamentalist Christians who thinks the Bible is the inspired Word of God. Okay, I'm a fair man," he continues, looking at his watch. "We have a little extra time. Why don't you take a moment and prove to the rest of the class that the Bible is not filled with fables?"

What has the professor just done? In one quick move, he has cleverly shifted the burden of proof back on you, the student. This is unfair, because *you* have not made any claim. *He* is the one who is expressing a view. It's up to him to defend it. He's the teacher, after all.

Don't take the bait. Falling into this trap is nearly always fatal. The professor is trying to get you to do his job. Don't let it happen.

Instead, when you find yourself facing any form of the "Why don't you try to prove me wrong?" challenge, shift the burden back where it belongs, on the one who made the claim. Respond this way: "Professor, I actually haven't said anything about my own view, so you're just guessing right now. For all you know, I could be on your side. More to the point, my own view is irrelevant. It doesn't really matter what I believe. *Your* ideas are on the table, not *mine*. I'm just a student trying to learn. I'm asking for clarification and wondering if you have good reasons. That's all."

If he gives an answer, thank him for explaining himself and either ask another question or let it go for the time being. You have done the best you can under the circumstances.

The "professor's ploy" is to shift the burden of proof from himself to someone else. He demands that others defend views they have not expressed even though he is the one who has made specific claims. He tries to sidestep his responsibility, but the burden of proof is still his.

Do not be afraid to question your professors. Challenge them on your terms, though, not theirs. And do it with grace, respect, and tact. Remember, you don't have to be the expert on every subject. If you keep the burden of proof on the other side when the other person is making the claim, it takes the pressure off you but still allows you to direct the conversation.

GETTING OUT OF THE "HOT SEAT"

There's a further advantage of Columbo. I call it "getting out of the hot seat." Sometimes we're afraid we do not have enough information or are not quick enough on our feet to keep up with a fast talker in an intense discussion. The fear of getting in over our heads is enough to keep us from saying anything at all. We especially dread the possibility of being embarrassed by some aggressive critic blasting us with arguments, opinions, or information we are not equipped to handle.

In this circumstance, the tactical approach really shines. Columbo questions help you easily manage the conversation even when you sense you are overmatched.

First, don't feel under pressure to immediately answer every question asked or every point made, especially when someone else is coming on strong. Instead, practice a little conversational aikido. Let them keep coming at you, but use their aggressive energy to your advantage.

The minute you feel overmatched, buy yourself some time by shifting from persuasion mode to fact-finding mode. Don't try to argue your own case yet. Instead, ask probing clarification questions and ask for reasons (your first two Columbo questions). Say something like this:

> It sounds like you know a lot more about this than I do, and you have some interesting ideas. The problem is, this is all new information for me. I wonder if you could do me a favor. I really want to understand your points, but you need to slow down so I can get them right. Would you take a moment to carefully explain your view and also your reasons for it to help me understand better?

These questions show you are interested in taking the other person's view seriously. They also buy you valuable time. Make sure you understand the ideas. Write them down if you need to. When all your questions have been answered, end the conversation by saying the magic words: "*Let me think about it.* Maybe we can talk more later."

These words — Let me think about it — are like magic because once you say them, you free yourself from any obligation to respond further at the moment. All the pressure is gone because you have already pleaded ignorance. You have no obligation to answer, refute, or reply once you have admitted you are outgunned and need to give the issue more thought.

Think for a moment how useful this approach is. Instead of trying to resist the force of another's attack, you step aside and let him have the floor. You invite him to make his case. However, he must do it slowly and clearly so you'll have an opportunity to fully understand his point.

Next, on your own, at your leisure, when the pressure is off, do your homework. Research the issue — maybe even enlisting others in the process — and come back better prepared next time. You might even want to start a notebook. Open a computer file and record the question and its details from your notes. Then begin to craft a response based on your research.

Finally, review what you have written. Rehearse your response out loud a few times, or role-play with a friend. If your discussion was just part of a chance meeting, you may not be able to revisit the topic with the same person. But when the issue comes up with someone else, you'll be ready. You'll own that question.

When you face a new challenge, start another entry and go through the same steps. You'll be surprised how soon your expanding notebook will cover the basic issues. There aren't that many.

The key here is to get out of the hot seat, but still stay engaged by deftly shifting control of the conversation back to you while shifting the spotlight — and the pressure — back on him. It's not retreat; it's just a different type of engagement. It greatly reduces your anxiety level, strengthens your confidence, and gives you an education so that you can be more effective the next time around.

If you take this approach, no egos are at stake, so there are no losers. You are simply asking the more aggressive person to give you his best shot. Essentially, you are inviting him to do what he wanted to do in the first place, beat you up. You're just giving him the opportunity to do a complete job.

Now let me ask you a question. Is there any Christian you know — even the most retiring, shy, bashful, timid, or reserved — who is unable to do this? Is there anyone who cannot say, "Oh, so you want to beat me up? Fine with me. Just do it slowly and thoroughly." There isn't. This is easy. Anyone can do it. This little technique will allow the most skittish Christian to tame a tyrant. It really works.

WHAT WE LEARNED IN THIS CHAPTER

First, we learned the second use of the Columbo tactic. It is based on the notion that people should be able to give reasons for important things they think are true. Instead of letting our critics have a free ride, we make them defend their own beliefs — or unbelief, as the case may be.

I called this move "reversing the burden of proof." In any dispute, the person who advances an opinion, claim, or point of view has the job of defending it. It's not your duty to prove him wrong. It's his duty to prove himself right. Our second Columbo question, "How did you come to that conclusion?" applies the burden-of-proof rule.

When someone says to you, "The Bible's been changed so many times," or "You don't need God to have morality," or "There's an infinite number of universes, and ours just happens to be the one that looks designed," don't retreat in silence. Instead, simply raise your eyebrows and say, "Oh? How did you come to that conclusion?"

Second, we learned how a basic argument was structured. Opinions alone are not proof. A person giving a real argument does more than just state her opinion. She supports her point of view with evidence and reasons much like the walls of a house support the roof. Roofs are useless when they are on the ground. In the same way, it's not enough for someone to contradict your view by simply telling a story. An alternate explanation is not a refutation. The new option must not only be possible, or even plausible, but it must be more likely (all things considered) than the idea you are offering.

Next, we learned how to deal with the "professor's ploy," a common move used by others to escape the burden of proof. There are two important principles here. One, do not allow yourself to get caught in a power play when you are overmatched. Instead, use your tactics. Two, refuse to shoulder the burden of proof when you have not made a claim. The Columbo tactic comes to your rescue in each of these situations.

Finally, we learned how to use Columbo to keep ourselves out of the "hot seat." When we find that we are overmatched by a fast talker in an intense discussion, we practice a little "verbal aikido" by shifting from argument mode to fact-finding mode. We ask probing clarification questions instead of trying to win our case. Then we use the magic phrase "Let me think about it." Once we understand the other person's point of view, we work on the issues later, on our own, when the pressure is off.

CHAPTER FIVE

STEP THREE: USING COLUMBO TO LEAD THE WAY

UP until now, we have talked about using the Columbo tactic in a very particular way. We have used friendly questions to gather two types of information: a person's view and his reasons for it. One of the advantages of this approach, we noted, was that it is largely a passive enterprise. We put nothing on the line. Since there is nothing for us to defend, there is no pressure.

By contrast, the third use of Columbo takes us more on the offensive, yet in an inoffensive way. We ask a different kind of question, sometimes called a "leading question." As the name suggests, leading questions take the other person in the direction we want them to go. Think of yourself as an archer shooting at a target. Questions are your arrows. Your target will be different in different situations. Sometimes your goal will be to defeat what you think is a bad argument or a flawed point of view. Your questions will be "aimed" at that purpose. Or you may want to use questions to indirectly explain or advance your own ideas. Sometimes you will set up the terms of the conversation using questions to put you in a more beneficial position for your next move.

In each of these cases, questions accomplish two things that mere statements cannot. Every time you ask a question and get a favorable response, the person is telling you he *understands* the point you're making and *agrees* with it, at least provisionally. He takes another step forward with you in the thinking process.

Ultimately, we want to win someone over to our point of view. But we don't want to force our opinions. Instead, we want to persuade. When the steps to a conclusion are both clear and reasonable, it is much easier to convince someone because he can see the route clearly. He can even retrace it on his own if he wants to. With each question, we lead him closer toward our destination. In this way, we bring him along on the journey.

> When you get approvals for each successive link in the process of reasoning, you move the conversation in the direction **you** have in mind. In that way, you carefully guide the other person to your conclusion.

There are a handful of ways that this third use of Columbo can work. Generally, your leading questions will be used to inform, persuade, set up the terms, or refute. Let me show you how this tactic plays out in specific examples.

THE QUESTION

As you step out as an ambassador for Christ, inevitably you will be asked what I call *"the* question." It's one of the most important questions anyone can ask, but it's also one of the most difficult because the correct answer — a simple "yes" — would be wildly misleading.

The leading New Age author Deepak Chopra put *the* question to me this way in a national TV debate: "You're saying that people who don't believe just like you are going to Hell?" Someone once said if you word the question right, you can win any debate. Dr. Chopra's was a classic case in point. A simple "yes" would be the correct answer, but it actually would distort the truth.

Dr. Chopra's question was not meant to clarify a theological point. Instead, in the gamesmanship of the moment, his challenge was intended to discredit me with the audience. If I answered directly — "Yes, people who do not believe in Jesus are going to Hell" — the debate would be over. Chopra's query would have succeeded in painting me with an ugly stereotype. Viewers would not hear Jesus offering reprieve and rescue from a judgment they each will face. Instead, they would hear conceit and condescension from a "fundamentalist" wishing Hell on anyone who doesn't see things his way.

The third use of the Columbo tactic helps us out of this dilemma, but there's a hitch. Remember from chapter 1 that the first responsibility of an ambassador is knowledge — an accurately informed mind. Knowing that people need to trust in Jesus or face judgment, though, is not enough. Since this truth does not give an accurate sense of *why* Jesus matters, God seems petty, pitching people into Hell because of some inconsequential detail of Christian theology.

The hitch is this: You have to know *why* Jesus is the only way before it is helpful to tell people *that* he is the only way. Without that knowledge, the third step of Columbo will not help you on this issue.

In Chopra's case, I decided to sidestep his challenge rather than try to resolve such a delicate issue with a sound byte. Instead, I used his question as a springboard to make a different point, one I thought was strategic to my own purposes.[1]

I addressed the issue of why Jesus is the only way again when the question came up during a book promotion at a local Barnes & Noble store. I met an attorney there who didn't understand why he, a Jew, needed Jesus. He believed in God, and he was doing his best to live a moral life. It seemed to him that those were the important things — how he lived, not what he believed. Here is how I used Columbo questions to lead him to a proper understanding of the cross.

"Let me ask you a question," I began. "Do you think people who commit moral crimes ought to be punished?"

"Well, since I'm a prosecuting attorney," he chuckled, "I guess I do."

"Good. So do I. Now, a second question: Have *you* ever committed any moral crimes?"

He paused for a moment. This was getting personal. "Yes," he nodded, "I guess I have."

"So have I," I offered candidly, agreeing with him again. "But that puts us both in a tight spot, doesn't it? We both believe people who do bad things should be punished, and we both believe we're guilty on that score." I waited a moment for the significance to sink in. "Do you know what I call that?" I asked. "I call that bad news."

In less than 60 seconds I had accomplished a remarkable thing with my two questions. I didn't have to convince this man he was a sinner. *He was telling me.* I didn't have to convince him he deserved to be punished. *He was telling me.*

I was tapping into a deep intuition every person shares: knowledge of his own guilt and a realization that his guilt should be punished. And I didn't do it arrogantly or in an obnoxious, condescending way. I freely admitted I was in the same trouble he was.

Now that we agreed on the problem, it was time to give the solution. (This is where the "knowledge" part of the ambassador equation is so vital.)

"This is where Jesus comes in," I explained. "We both know we're guilty. That's the problem. So God offers a solution: a pardon, free of charge. But clemency is on his terms, not ours. Jesus is God's means of pardon. He personally paid the penalty in our place. He took the rap for our crimes. No one else did that. Only Jesus. Now we have a choice to make. Either we take the pardon and go free, or we turn it down and pay for our crimes ourselves."

In this conversation I handled an awkward question by combining two things: my knowledge of what Jesus accomplished on the cross and the Columbo tactic. My questions led the attorney, step-by-step, to an answer to his question.

TELL THEM SOMETHING THEY KNOW

The most powerful questions — and the most persuasive — are the ones that help people recall what they already know. In the case of the attorney, I asked key questions to cause his own intuitions about guilt and punishment to rise to the surface. The approach was powerful because I didn't have to persuade him of some foreign idea. I merely connected the dots.

This was true of Shannon, an American college student living in Germany whom I met on a train from Normandy to Paris. Shannon had been raised in a Christian home. She'd been educated at a Christian college and had what she described as a "strong relationship with the Lord." Still, like the attorney, she was perplexed by the idea that others were lost apart from trust in Christ.

"What about someone who believes in God?" she asked. "What about the person who is sincerely following his own religion and trying to be the best person he can be?" I hear these kinds of questions from non-Christians all the time. But I also hear them with surprising frequency from believers. I suspected Shannon already knew enough to answer her own question. She simply had not pieced it together.

"Why should anyone become a Christian in the first place?" I asked. "You and I are Christians. What benefit does putting our trust in Jesus give us?"

"Jesus saves us," she answered.

"From what?"

"He saves us from our sins."

"Right. You might say we have a spiritual disease called sin, and Jesus did something on the cross that healed the disease." She nodded.

"Can simply believing in God heal that disease?"

"No," she said after thinking a moment.

"Can trying our best to be a good person heal it, or being really religious, or even being completely sincere? Can any of those things forgive our sin?" She shook her head. No, none of those things in themselves could take away our guilt. "We'd still be dying from our spiritual disease, wouldn't we?" I said. She agreed.

Then I simply connected the dots for her. "If religion, or sincerity, or 'doing our best' cannot save *you and me*, then how can any of those things save *someone else*? Either Jesus rescues us by taking the punishment for our sin on himself, or we are not saved and we have to pay for our own crimes. It's no more complicated than that."

Notice two things about this conversation. First, I gave Shannon no new information. I just reminded her of things she already knew, but had not related to her own concern. Second, I did it almost entirely with questions.

TURNING THE TABLES

The third use of Columbo can help you get out of a different kind of tough situation. Sometimes you may need to use questions to set up the conversation in a way that is most favorable to you.

I have a friend who is a deeply committed Christian woman and whose boss is a lesbian. That in itself isn't the problem. My friend has the maturity to know that you can't expect non-Christians to live like Christians. The difficulty is that her boss wanted to know what my friend thought about homosexuality.

> If you are placed in a situation where you suspect your convictions will be labeled intolerant, bigoted, narrow-minded, or judgmental, use Columbo to turn the tables.

When someone asks for your personal views about a controversial issue, preface your remarks with a question that sets the stage — in your favor — for your response. Say, "You know, this is actually a very personal question you're asking. I don't mind answering, but before I do, I want to know if it's safe to offer my views. So let me ask you a question: Do you consider yourself a tolerant person or an intolerant person on issues like this? Is it safe to give my opinion, or are you going to judge me for my point of view? Do you respect diverse points of view, or do you condemn others for convictions that differ from your own?" Now when you give your point of view, it's going to be very difficult for anyone to call you intolerant or judgmental without looking guilty, too.

This line of questioning trades on an important bit of knowledge: There is no neutral ground when it comes to the tolerance question. Everybody has a point of view she thinks is right, and everybody passes judgment at some point or another. The Christian gets pigeonholed as the judgmental one, but everyone else is judging, too, even people who consider themselves relativists.

I call this the passive-aggressive tolerance trick.[2] The key to understanding this trick is knowing that everyone thinks his own beliefs are correct. If people didn't think their beliefs were true, they wouldn't believe them. They'd believe something else and think *that* was true.

If you have already been labeled intolerant by someone, ask, "What do you mean by that?" This, of course, is an example of the first Columbo question. Though I already have a pretty good idea of what the person means when she says I'm intolerant, asking this question flushes out her definition of "intolerant" and sets the stage — in my favor — for the next two questions. Here's how it looks:

"You're intolerant."

"Can you tell me what you mean by that? Why would you consider me an intolerant person?"

"Well, it's clear you think you're right and everyone who disagrees with you is wrong."

"I guess I do think my views are correct. It's always possible I could be mistaken, but in this case I don't think I am. But what about you? You seem to be disagreeing with me. Do you think your own views are right?"[3]

"Yes, I think I'm right, too. But I'm not intolerant. You are."

"That's the part that confuses me. *Why is it when I think I'm right, I'm intolerant, but when you think you're right, you're just right?* What am I missing?"

Of course, *you* are not missing anything; she is. Her move is simple name-calling. Labeling you as intolerant is no different than calling you ugly. One is an attack on your *looks*. The other is an attack on your *character*. Neither is useful in helping you understand the merits of any *idea* you may be discussing.[4]

> The quickest way to deal with a personal attack is to simply point it out with a question. When someone goes after you rather than your argument, ask, "I'm a little confused about your response. Even if you were right about my character, could you explain to me exactly what that has to do with this issue?"

EXPLOITING A WEAKNESS OR A FLAW

You might have noticed something unique about how I dealt with the tolerance trick. My questions went beyond positioning myself in a more favorable way in our conversation. This time I also used Columbo questions to challenge the other person's ideas. Once you have a clear understanding of what a person thinks and why he thinks it, you can move on to this step: using questions to subtly expose a weakness or a flaw, or to uproot difficulties or problems you detect in his view.

I stumbled upon a wonderful example of this while reading *Icons of Evolution*, the fine critique of Darwinism by Jonathan Wells.

The following dialogue is an example of one student's gentle use of the third step in the Columbo tactic:

Teacher: Okay, let's start today's lesson with a quick review. Yesterday I talked about homology [how different organisms show remarkable similarity in the structure of some of their body parts]. Homologous features, such as the vertebrate limbs shown in your textbook, provide us with some of our best evidence that living things have evolved from common ancestors.

Student (raising hand): I know you went over this yesterday, but I'm still confused. How do we know whether features are homologous?

Teacher: Well, if you look at vertebrate limbs, you can see that even though they're adapted to perform different functions, their bone patterns are structurally similar.

Student: But you told us yesterday that even though an octopus eye is structurally similar to a human eye, the two are not homologous.

Teacher: That's correct. Octopus and human eyes are not homologous because their common ancestor did not have such an eye.

Student: So regardless of similarity, features are not homologous unless they are inherited from a common ancestor?

Teacher: Yes, now you're catching on.

Student (looking puzzled): Well, actually, I'm still confused. You say homologous features provide some of our best evidence for common ancestry. But before we can tell whether features are homologous, we have to know whether they came from a common ancestor.

Teacher: That's right.

Student (scratching head): I must be missing something. It sounds as though you're saying that we know features are derived from a common ancestor because they're derived from a common ancestor. Isn't that circular reasoning?[5]

Here's another example of how to use Columbo to expose a weakness or a flaw. Let's revisit the conversation with our professor from chapter 4. In that section, we learned to avoid being taken in by what I called the "professor's ploy" by asking for reasons for his own view, in this case that the Bible was just a bunch of myths.

He might answer, "I know the Bible is a myth because it has miracles in it." This bit of valuable information sets up the next series of questions:

"And why does that mean the Bible is myth or fable?"

"Because miracles don't happen."

"How do you know that?"

"Because science has proven that miracles don't happen."

Now, I happen to know that science has proven nothing of the sort, nor can it. Since science only measures the natural world, it is not capable of ruling out anything, even in principle, in the supernatural realm.[6] Armed with this information, I can now ask the decisive question: "Professor, would you please explain to me exactly how the methods of science have disproved the possibility of supernatural events?"

The professor has no place to go at this point because no such scientific proof exists. Science has never *advanced* any empirical evidence to show that supernatural events cannot happen. Instead, science (and the professor) has *assumed*, prior to the evidence (i.e., *a priori*), according to naturalistic philosophy, that miracles are impossible.[7] Thus, any "historical" reference to supernatural signs is either a myth or a fable. Your simple question — and the long silence that follows it — does all the work necessary to make your point.

> One of the advantages of the Columbo tactic is not having to assert something you want someone else to believe. You aren't taking the burden of proof on yourself. Instead, you accomplish your goal in an entirely different — and more powerful — way. You use questions to make the point for you.

This last step is more demanding because you have to be able to see some weakness in the person's argument before you can work with it. How do you find the flaw? There is no special formula for making this discovery. The key is to pay close attention to the answer to the question, "How did you come to that conclusion?" Then, ask yourself if the person's conclusion is justified by the evidence he gives.

Remember, an argument is like a house whose roof is supported by walls. In this step of Columbo you want to find out if the walls (the reasons or evidence) are strong enough to hold up the roof (the person's point of view).

Look, observe, reflect. Maybe your friend's comments have tipped you off to some problem with his view. Is there a misstep, a non sequitur,[8] a fallacy, or a failing of some sort? Can you challenge any underlying assumptions that might be faulty? Whatever you discover, be sure to address the problem with a question, not a statement.

STUMPED OR STALLED OUT?

Getting to the third use of Columbo requires insight that the first two Columbo questions do not. You need to know the specific direction you want the conversation to go, the precise purpose you want to accomplish with your leading questions. Do you want to use your questions to clarify a point? To convey new information? To expose a weakness? You have to know which target to aim at before you can continue.

This skill takes time to develop, so don't be surprised — or discouraged — if you find yourself stalled out at first. It's not always easy to flush out the error in someone's thinking or to maneuver in conversation using questions instead of statements. This takes a little practice, but in time, you'll improve. In the second half of this book, "Part Two: Finding the Flaws," I give you a handful of tactics to make this easier.

If you find you don't have the resources to go further in a discussion or if you sense the person is losing interest, *don't feel compelled to force the conversation.* Let the encounter die a natural death and move on. Consider it a fruitful, interactive learning experience nonetheless.

Remember, as an ambassador for Christ, you don't have to hit a home run in every conversation. You don't even have to get on base, in my opinion. As I mentioned in chapter 2, sometimes just getting up to bat will do. Your first two Columbo questions — "What do you mean by that?" and "How did you come to that conclusion?" — will help you get in the game. The rest will come in time.

> We may spend hours helping someone carefully work through an issue without ever mentioning God, Jesus, or the Bible. This does not mean we aren't advancing the kingdom. It is always a step in the right direction when we help others think more carefully. If nothing else, it gives them tools to assess the bigger questions that eventually come up.

INNOCENT AS DOVES

I mentioned at the beginning of the chapter that the third use of Columbo takes us on the offensive. The danger, of course, is that we *become* offensive when we go *on* the offensive. These are two different things. Yes, we want to be able to point out weaknesses in a view (go *on* the offensive). But we don't want to seem pushy, condescending, or smug (*being* offensive). How do we maintain balance?

Jesus offered this advice: "Be shrewd as serpents, and innocent as doves" (Matthew 10:16). I think one of the things he had in mind was that we should be clever in our approach, yet remain innocent in our appearance.

Here's how Jesus' insight might apply. Sometimes the best way to disagree with someone is not to face the issue head-on, but to soften the challenge by using an indirect approach. You can cushion your third use of Columbo a couple of ways.

For one, think about using the phrase "Have you considered" to introduce your concern, then offering a different view that gently questions the person's beliefs or confronts a weakness with his argument. Here are some examples:

- "Have you ever considered ... that if the Bible were 'merely written by men' it would be very hard to account for fulfilled prophecy? How would you explain that?"
- "Have you ever considered ... the difficulty involved with removing something like the teaching on reincarnation from every existing handwritten copy of the New Testament in circulation in the Roman world by the fourth century? How is this physically possible?"
- "Have you ever considered ... that the existence of evil is actually evidence for the existence of God, not against it?"[9]
- "Have you ever considered ... that if partial-birth abortion is okay, it's going to be hard to condemn infanticide, since the baby's location — partially out of the womb (partial-birth abortion) or completely out (infanticide) — is the only difference between the two? Doesn't location seem irrelevant to the baby's value?"
- "Have you ever considered ... that if Jesus was wrong about being the only way of salvation, it is difficult to call him a good

man, a prophet, or a wise religious teacher? What do you think about that problem?"

Another way to soften your challenge is to phrase your concern as a request for clarification. Begin by asking, "Can you clear this up for me?" or "Can you help me understand this?" Then offer your objection in a way that gently challenges the belief or confronts the weakness you think you see in the argument. Consider the gentle approach of the following questions:

- Can you clear this up for me? If Jesus' divinity was an invention of the church in the early fourth century, how do you explain all the references to a divine Christ in literature written before that time?
- Can you help me understand this? If there is no evidence that life came from non-life (abiogenesis) — that life spontaneously arose from inanimate matter to kick off the sequence of evolution — and there is much evidence against it, how can we say that Darwinian evolution is fact?
- Can you help me with something that confuses me? How does having a 'burning in the bosom' about the Book of Mormon give adequate evidence that this book is from God when people have similar reasons — a strong conviction from God in response to prayer — for rejecting it?
- Can you clear this up for me? If homosexuality is truly natural, then why did nature give homosexual men bodies designed for reproductive sex with women and then give them desires for sex with men? Why would nature give desires for one type of sex, but a body for another?

One of the reasons this approach is so attractive is that it emphasizes respect for the person you disagree with. First, you have made an effort (with your first two Columbo questions) to understand her viewpoint. Next, you ask, "Do you mind if I ask a couple of questions about what you've told me?" or "Would you consider an alternative, or be willing to look at another angle?" By soliciting permission to disagree, you make the encounter more amicable. You also stay in the driver's seat.

There is one more way to soften your approach that, strictly speaking, may not involve Columbo (because it doesn't always use a question). Even so, it may serve a valuable tactical purpose. You may find yourself in a situation where either you can't think of a question or where it would seem awkward or contrived to use a question rather than simply stating your view.

In these circumstances, you need a genial way to introduce your point. Here are some recommendations you might want to consider:

- Let me suggest an alternative, and tell me if you think it's an improvement. If not, you can tell me why you think your option is better.
- I wouldn't characterize it that way. Here's what I think may be a better or more accurate way to look at it. Tell me what you think.
- I don't think that's going to work, and I'd like to suggest why. Is that okay with you?
- I'm not sure I agree with the way you put it. Think about this ...

These statements protect you in an additional way. When you say something like, "It's my understanding that ..." or "This is the way it seems to me," then explain your position and invite a response, you indicate you are provisional in your claims. Yes, you have convictions, but they are open to discussion.

This is not only an implicit act of humility, but it also gives you a margin of safety. It may turn out that you have missed something that your friend uncovers in the process of conversation. If you discover that your own ideas are compromised in some way, this could be embarrassing if you expressed them in a dogmatic, uncompromising way to begin with. Furthermore, you have little psychological liberty to adjust your views.[10]

NARRATING THE DEBATE

Many people you talk to will struggle when you turn the tables by asking them to give evidence for the claims they make. When a person has not thought much about his own assertions, dodging your questions may be his only recourse. He may try to change the subject or reassert his point in other ways.

When this happens, it may be helpful for you to "narrate the debate." Take a moment to step outside of the conversation, in a sense, and describe to your friend the turn the discussion has taken. This will help him (and others listening in) see how he's gotten off course.

You can say something like, "I want you to notice what has just happened. First you made a fairly controversial statement, and I asked you a couple of questions about it. So far, you haven't answered them. Instead, you have taken off in another direction. Before we move on to a new topic, would it be okay with you if we finish the old one? I really am interested in your response."

Don't let your friend get off the hook by dodging the issues. This approach keeps the burden on him while keeping the conversation cordial. Encourage the other person to clarify himself. Forcing him to face the music may be the first step toward a change of mind.

> When a cherished view is at stake, it's not unusual for people to raise empty objections — objections that initially sound worthwhile, but simply can't be defended once examined. Questions aimed at undermining the view often reveal a lack of substance behind the bluster.

WHAT WE LEARNED IN THIS CHAPTER

In this chapter we learned how to employ Columbo to take us in an entirely new direction. Instead of using questions to gather information, we discovered that questions can be very effective to lead someone in the direction we want the conversation to go. Such "leading questions" often work better than statements to explain our view, to set up the discussion in a way that makes it easier for us to make our point, to soften our challenge to another's view, or to indirectly expose a flaw in the other's thinking.

Unlike the first two uses of Columbo, this one requires knowledge of some kind. When we know what we want to accomplish (e.g., to inform, to persuade, to set up the terms, or to refute), we can use leading questions to achieve our purpose. This is a skill that develops over time, so if you stall out at first, don't be discouraged. Instead of trying to force a conversation you don't have the resources to pursue, you can simply move on, knowing you have done the best that you could for the moment.

If someone's thinking is flawed, the key to finding the error is to listen carefully to the reasons and then ask if the conclusions follow from the evidence. Point out errors with questions rather than statements. You might soften your challenge by phrasing your concern as a request for clarification or by suggesting an alternative with the words "Have you considered . . ." before offering your own ideas.

CHAPTER SIX

PERFECTING COLUMBO

WE have spent quite a bit of time focusing on a single tactic. I have taken this time because Columbo is so important. It is central to every tactic that follows.

If you have been practicing what we have covered, you have already discovered how handy Columbo can be. You're learning how to advance the dialogue for spiritual ends without seeming pushy. You're realizing that asking simple questions is an almost effortless way to have courteous conversations with others, even if you strongly disagree with their ideas.

You might have noticed, though, that it is difficult to be clever on command. Sometimes it is hard to think of new things on the spur of the moment. You may be able to get conversations started, but then you get bogged down.

To perfect any new skill takes time and practice. If you were just beginning to learn a sport such as tennis, some of your time would be spent practicing the basics (a forehand or a volley, for instance). Then you would get feedback from someone else who could help you improve your technique. Similarly, as you begin to implement your tactical game plan using Columbo, you might wonder if there is something you can do to improve your technique, a way to practice before the pressure is on.

You might also notice something else. You might discover that you are not the only one who can use questions to navigate tactically in conversations. Others — including those who disagree with you — know how to do this, too, and some are very skilled at it.

In this chapter, I would like to coach you in specific ways to improve your Columbo skill. I also want to show you how to defend against the Columbo tactic when someone else uses it on you. Finally, I will recount a conversation I had with a waitress at a Seattle restaurant because it is a good example of how the various elements of Columbo come together in a single encounter.

IMPROVING YOUR COLUMBO SKILL

Initially, you will not be quick on your feet with responses like the ones in the examples I have given in previous chapters. Instead, you may find that your best ideas come when your head is clear and you are not under pressure to respond immediately. In any encounter, there are two different times when the pressure is off: before the conversation begins and after it's over. Those are perfect times to focus on improving your technique.

Peter reminds us to always be "ready to make a defense to everyone who asks you to give an account for the hope that is in you" (1 Peter 3:15). There are three specific things you can do to "ready" yourself to respond. You can *anticipate* beforehand what might come up. You can *reflect* afterward on what took place. And in both cases you can *practice* the responses you think of during these reflective moments so you will be prepared for the next opportunity.

First, think about conversations you might have about your convictions and try to anticipate obstacles you might encounter. Then think of Columbo questions in advance. Work on an issue or a question that people frequently ask you about or that has stumped you in the past. Brainstorm a handful of straightforward response questions that might put you in the driver's seat of those conversations. Imagine what it would look like to have a dialogue using your questions. This small bit of advance preparation takes a little work, but can be very effective. The next time you face those challenges, the responses will be right at your fingertips.

> Always try to anticipate the rejoinders or coun-
> terarguments the other side might raise. Take
> these rejoinders seriously, stating them fairly
> and clearly — even convincingly. Then refute
> them in advance. This tactic removes the objec-
> tions before they're raised. It's as if you're saying,
> "I know what you're thinking and it's not going to
> work. Here's why."

Second, after each encounter, take some time for self-assessment. I have made it a habit to immediately reflect on how I could have done better. It has become second nature. How did I do? Could I have asked better questions or maneuvered differently in the conversation? What were my missteps? How could I improve? With the pressure off, alternatives occur to me.

This is where the Ambassador Model from chapter 1 comes in handy. When I ask myself about the three skills of an ambassador — knowledge, an accurately informed mind; wisdom, an artful method; and character, an attractive manner — I have something specific to focus on. Did I know enough about the issue, or do I need to brush up on something for next time? Could I have maneuvered with more tactical wisdom in the conversation? Was my manner attractive? Did I act with grace, kindness, and patience?

You can do the same thing. Ask how you could have phrased questions more effectively or conducted yourself differently in the conversation. If a friend was with you during the encounter, enlist her help. As a bystander in the conversation, how did she think you were coming across?

This kind of assessment is not hard at all and can be a lot of fun. When you go back and think about an encounter, it prepares you for your next opportunity. The next time around, these new ideas will quickly come to mind.

Finally, when you think of a new idea or approach, practice it out loud. I do this constantly. I try to anticipate the twists and turns my new approach might take and how I would respond to possible comebacks. If I think of something, I practice it out loud. I say, "I could have said this …," and then I play out the alternative. Often I'll write down my thoughts and review them later. If I'm with a friend, I ask him to role-play with me. He may think of moves on either side of the conversation that haven't occurred to me. Also, when we work on it together, we both learn from the experience.

Sometimes I practice this way when I'm alone in the car listening to talk radio. After listening to a few comments by the host or a caller, I turn the volume down and then pretend it is my job to respond to what was said. It's almost like being on live radio, except if I say something foolish, no one hears it.

Practice like this increases your practical experience. It places you in an actual dialogue in a way that is completely safe. Then, when these issues come up in real-life encounters, you'll be ready because you have already rehearsed your responses.

This is the way I prepare every time I'm interviewed on radio or TV, or every time I'm in a campus debate or a public "cross-fire" situation. It may sound to listeners like I am clever or quick on my feet, but this is not the case. Usually, my answers are not spontaneous at all, even when the conversation takes an unpredictable turn. If I have predicted the turn in advance and prepared for it, then I am not caught by surprise.

This is the same way political candidates prepare for televised debates or comedians prepare to be "spontaneously" funny on late-night talk shows. You will probably never be in a situation quite like one of these, but that doesn't mean you can't learn from their methods.

> When you think of improving your Columbo skill, remember this important truth: Even people who don't usually like taking tests don't mind them at all when they know the answers to the questions.

As you work on developing your own proficiency, I think you will discover something that I have learned. There are two things that will help generate the courage you'll need to face a challenging situation: preparation and action. Being prepared will give you confidence, but eventually you must engage. Interacting with others face-to-face is *the most effective way* to improve your abilities as an ambassador.

Let me give you some examples of things I wish I would have said during a conversation, but didn't think of until after I'd worked through the steps I described above.

In chapter 1, I mentioned a conversation I had with an actor's wife about animal rights. Here is how that evening ended. As I stood at the door thanking the hosts, I asked one last question about our discussion. It is a question I ask all animal rights advocates if I get the opportunity: "Where do you stand on abortion?" I had no intention of arguing further. I just wanted to know her views, for the record. To my way of thinking, the answer to this question is a measure of an animal rights person's intellectual integrity.

She gave me the same answer I have received from every single person I have asked who held her views. "I'm pro-abortion," she said. Then she clarified, "I'm not actually *for* abortion, I just don't believe any unwanted children should be allowed to come into the world." I thanked her for her candid answer and departed.

Driving home, I couldn't help thinking about her final comments. I was sure I had missed an opportunity, but what was it? Suddenly I realized what was wrong with her response. Not wanting to bring unwanted children into the world may be a legitimate reason for birth control, but it has nothing to do with abortion. When a women is pregnant, the child is already "in the world," so to speak. The human being already exists; he or she is just hidden from view inside the mother's womb. This woman's response assumed that before making the journey down the birth canal, the baby simply does not exist.

This was a weakness that could be exploited with a question. I could have responded to her comment by asking, "Do you think children ought to be allowed to *stay* in the world if they are unwanted?" The answer to this question must always be "yes," unless someone wants to affirm infanticide, something I'm sure this woman would never do. The door is now open to a final query, the leading question that properly frames the debate: "The issue with abortion, then, isn't whether the child is wanted, but whether or not a woman already *has* a child when she is pregnant, isn't it?"[1]

Here's another example of an opportunity I missed. Once in a dorm lounge at Ohio State University, a student asked me about the Bible and homosexuality. When I cited some texts, he quickly dismissed them. "People twist the Bible all the time to make it say whatever they want," he sniffed.

I don't recall my specific response to him that evening. I do remember, though, that I was not satisfied with my answer. On the drive back to my hotel, I gave the conversation a little more thought. I realized it made little sense to argue with his comment as it stood. It was uncontroversial. People *do* twist Bible verses all the time. It is one of my own chief complaints. Something else was going on though, and I couldn't put my finger on it at first.

Suddenly it dawned on me. The student's point wasn't really that *some* people twist the Bible. His point was that *I* was twisting the Bible. Yet he hadn't demonstrated this. He had not shown where I'd gotten off track. Rather, he didn't like my point, so he dismissed it with a some-people-twist-the-Bible dodge.

I quickly wrote out a short dialogue using questions (Columbo 1 and 2) intended to surface that problem. I also tried to anticipate his responses and how I would use them to advance my point (Columbo 3).

Here is what I came up with:

"People twist the Bible all the time to make it say whatever they want."

"Well, you're right about that. It bugs me, too. But your comment confuses me a little. What does it have to do with the point I just made about homosexuality?"

"Well, you're doing the same thing."

"Oh, so you think *I'm* twisting the Bible right now?"

"That's right."

"Okay. Now I understand what you were getting at, but I'm still confused."

"Why?"

"Because it seems to me you can't know that *I'm* twisting the Bible just by pointing out that *other* people have twisted it, can you?"

"What do you mean?"

"I mean that in *this* conversation you're going to have to do more than simply point out that other people twist the Bible. What do you think that might be?

"I don't know. What?"

"You need to show that *I'm* actually twisting the verses. Have you ever studied the passages I referred to?"

"No."

"Then how do you know I'm twisting them?"

A word of caution here. Once you learn Colombo, you'll realize how incapable most people are to answer for their own views. The temptation will be strong to use your tactical skill like a club. Don't give in to that urge.

> As a general rule, go out of your way to establish common ground. Whenever possible, affirm points of agreement. Take the most charitable read on the other person's motives, not the most cynical. Treat them the way you would like others to treat you if you were the one in the hot seat.

TURNABOUT: DEFENDING AGAINST COLUMBO

The proper use of Columbo depends to a large degree on the goodwill of the person using it. The purpose of our questions is not to confuse but to clarify — to clarify the issues in the discussion, to clarify our point, or to clarify some error we think the other person has made.

What do you do, though, when someone else begins to use Columbo against you, especially when you suspect that his motives are not so noble? How do you respond when you think another person's questions are intended to trap, manipulate, or humiliate you?

Before I answer this challenge, let me make a clarification. There is no risk when someone asks you either of the *first two* Columbo questions. We welcome the opportunity to clarify our views and then give our reasons for what we believe. The danger we need to guard against is the misuse of the *third* application of Columbo — leading questions.

The key to protecting yourself from what may be a Columbo ambush is to remind yourself that *you are in complete control of your own side of the conversation.* You have no obligation to cooperate with anyone trying to set you up with leading questions. Simply refuse to answer them, but do so in a cordial way.

Politely respond to unwelcome queries by saying, "Before we go further, let me say something. My sense is that you want to explain your point by using questions. That confuses me a bit because I'm not sure how I should respond. I think I'd rather you just state your own view directly. Then let me chew on it for a while and see what I think. Would that be all right with you?"

Notice, this is essentially the same maneuver discussed in chapter 4 to get you out of the hot seat. This response forces the other person to change his approach. He can still make his point, but you avoid being trapped.

WHEN A QUESTION IS NOT A QUESTION

Sometimes you will be asked a question that is not a question at all. Instead, it is a challenge in disguise. Consider this comment made to me by a UCLA graduate student: "What gives you the right to say someone else's religion is wrong?"

This is the kind of remark that can catch you completely off guard, leaving you slack-jawed and dumbfounded. There's a reason for your confusion. Even though the statement is *worded* like a question, you are pretty sure it isn't one. Instead, it is a vague challenge of some sort. Now what?

People ask questions for different reasons. Sometimes they ask a question because they're curious or confused. They want information they think you can provide. Other questions are "rhetorical," tossed out simply to stimulate thinking or move the conversation forward. No response from you is necessary, nor is one expected.

"What gives you the right ...?" is different. It's not really a question at all. There's no curiosity involved. Instead, it is a statement disguised as a question, a kind of goal-line stand meant to stop you in your tracks. "Who are you to say?" is another example, along with its cousin, "Who's to say?"

These challenges can easily put you on the defensive because it's pretty clear they are not requests for information, nor are they harmless rhetorical probes. The question from the UCLA student was in that category. It wasn't rhetorical, nor was it a mere pursuit of facts. It was a challenge. She was making a point with a question, but what was it?

The best way to navigate in this situation is simply to point out that the question is confusing. Our trusty "What do you mean by that?" is perfect here. You might also say, "I get the impression you think I've made a mistake here. Where did I go wrong?" This will force the person to rephrase her question as a statement, which is precisely what you want.

In my case, I told the UCLA student her "question" was confusing. Did she really want to talk about rights? Did she really want to know what my credentials were, or what authority I had to speak on these things? Clearly not.

Anyway, I wasn't laying claim to any authority, nor was I promoting my pedigree, academic or otherwise. The only rights I was appealing to were rational rights. I offered an argument that stands or falls on its own merits, not on the authority of the speaker.

> Who's to say? Ultimately, **the person who has the best reasons** is in the best position to say what is true and what is false. This is the way sound thinking has always worked.

I wanted the student to think about what she was really saying with her "question," then rephrase it in the form of a statement. The most important thing to remember about these questions is that behind them lurk strong opinions that are open to challenge if they can be flushed into the open. That's what I was after.

For example, "What gives you the right to say someone else's religion is wrong?" can be restated as "No one is justified saying one religious view is better than another." "Who's to say?" means "No one could ever know the truth about that," or "One answer is just as good as another." "Who are you to say?" usually means "You're wrong for saying someone else is wrong." (This last one is obviously contradictory, but you might not have noticed that problem if the claim remained hidden behind a question mark.)

Each of these is a strong assertion. And each is open to challenge, which is my point. The statement-question has power only when it's allowed to be played. If you force the implicit claim to come to the surface, the objection loses its luster, and you can address the real point lurking in the shadows.

A WORD ON STYLE

There are two basic executions of the Columbo tactic. The first is the bumbling approach of Lieutenant Columbo himself—halting, head-scratching, and apparently harmless. This tack should be easy for most of us because that's often how we feel when we're trying to gain a foothold in a conversation. The second is more confrontational and aggressive. It's the technique a lawyer uses in a courtroom.

The style you adopt in any conversation will depend on your goal. Do you want to persuade the other person, or do you want to refute him? Persuasion comes across as more friendly because your goal is to win the person, not necessarily to win the argument. By contrast, lawyers want to win the argument. In order to convince the jury, they must refute the defendant.

Since my goal is usually to persuade, in most conversations I adopt the genial approach of Lieutenant Columbo himself. I soften my challenge by introducing my questions with phrases like, "I'm just curious …," "Something about this thing bothers me …," "Maybe I'm missing something …," or "Maybe you can clear this up for me.…"

Sometimes, though, my purpose is not to persuade the person I differ with, but to persuade the ones who are listening. This is the situation I face in a debate. I realize there is little hope of winning my opponent. The audience, though, is generally more open-minded. If I can prove my challenger wrong, I can win many of those who are on the fence, as long as I mind my manners.

In informal debates, I can use either style, depending on the situation. If someone is squaring off with me when others are listening in, I might choose a refutation style for the sake of the bystanders. This is especially true if my challenger is belligerent and I have little confidence that he will be moved. Prudence dictates that I refute him and persuade the crowd. In a classroom setting, I usually have a better chance of influencing the students than I have of changing the professor. Even so, because I am a student in his class I would usually take a more indirect, laid-back approach as an act of courtesy.

SHEEPISH IN SEATTLE

Once in a restaurant in Seattle, I got into a chat about religion with the waitress serving my table. My general comments in favor of spirituality were met with an approving nod, but a shadow of disapproval crossed her face when I mentioned that some religious beliefs seemed foolish to me.

"That's oppressive," she said, "not letting people believe what they want to believe."

Now, much could be said about this challenge. For example, notice that she took my judgment on religious belief as a threat to personal liberty. I ignored that problem, though, and zeroed in on a more fundamental flaw.

"Do you think I'm wrong, then," I asked, using a variation of the first Columbo question.

At this she balked, unwilling to commit the same error she had just accused me of making. "No.... I'm not saying you're wrong. I'm just trying to ... to understand your view."

I chuckled. "It's okay if you think I'm wrong. Really, it doesn't bother me. I just wonder why you don't admit it? Look, if you *don't* think I'm wrong, then why are you correcting me? And if you *do* think I'm wrong, then why were you oppressing me?"

Of course, *I* didn't think her comment was oppressive, but now I was playing her rules against her. Boxed in, she faltered for a moment, then changed the subject. "All religions are basically the same, after all."

It was a parry—a stock retort. I suspect it had worked for her before, and now she was trying it on me. But I noticed something about the comment. She had just made a claim, and it was up to her to support it. It was time for another Columbo question.

"Religions are basically the same? Really? In what way?" I asked.

My question had a remarkable effect. I was amazed at the impact those simple words had on her. Her jaw fell slack, and her face went blank. She didn't know what to say. She had obviously not thought much about the details of other religions. If she had, she'd have known they are worlds apart. Why the empty claim, then, if she had no idea of its truth? I suspect she'd gotten away with it before.

Finally, after a long pause, she came up with one similarity: "Well, all religions teach you shouldn't kill people; you shouldn't murder."

In point of fact, many religions aren't concerned with morality at all. A distinctive of the great monotheistic religions is their concern about ethical conduct, but that's exceptional, not standard. All religions aren't basically the same. Instead of lecturing her about it, though, I used my questions.

"Consider this," I said. "Either Jesus is the Messiah or he isn't, right?"

She nodded. So far, so good.

"If he *isn't* the Messiah," I continued, "then the Christians are wrong and the Jews are right. If he *is* the Messiah, then the Jews are wrong and the Christians are right. So, one way or another, somebody's right and somebody's wrong. Under no circumstances can they both be 'basically the same,' can they?"

It was a straightforward line of thinking that yielded what should have been an uncontroversial conclusion. Yet she ignored my question, regrouped, then continued: "Well, no one can ever know the truth about religion."

This is another assertion that should never go unchallenged, so I calmly asked, "Why would you believe a thing like that?"

The turnabout caught her by surprise. She was used to asking this particular question, not answering it. I was violating the rules, asking her for a reason for her beliefs, and she wasn't prepared for the role change.

I waited patiently, not breaking the silence, not letting her off the hook. Finally, she ventured: "But the Bible has been changed and translated so many times over the centuries you can't trust it."

Notice two things about this response. First, she had changed the subject once again. The alleged corruption of the Bible had nothing to do with the possibility of knowing religious truth. Even if the Bible vanished from the face of the earth, knowledge of God could still be possible, at least in principle. Second, her dodge was in the form of another claim, an assertion that it was her job to defend, not my job to refute.

"How do you know the Bible's been changed?" I asked. "Have you actually studied the transmission of the ancient documents of the text of the Bible?"

Once again, the question stalled her. "No, I've never studied it," she finally said. This was a remarkable admission, given her confident contention just moments before. But she didn't seem the least bit bothered.

I didn't have the heart to say what I might have said in a case like this — "Then you're saying you are sure about something you really know nothing about." I might have added, "If you've never studied this, how do you know the Bible has been changed as you say?"

Instead, I simply told her I had studied the question extensively and the academic results were in. The manuscripts were accurate to over 99 percent precision. The Bible hadn't been changed.

She was surprised. "Really?"

By this point the waitress was running out of comebacks. She watched her options evaporate one by one and began to get uncomfortable. "I feel like you're backing me into a corner," she complained.

I wasn't trying to be unkind or to bully her intellectually. I listened to what she said and took her points seriously. Yet with each claim she made, I asked fair questions that she had no answers for. Apparently, she'd never given any thought to the opinions she held with such certainty. She was dumbfounded by the challenges and complained she was being cornered.

This young lady was like so many I have encountered. She knew all the popular slogans, but when fair Columbo questions eliminated foolish options, the truth began closing in on her. This dear person was speechless, not because I was clever, but because, I suspect, she'd never had to defend her own responses before.

When she says to Christians, "Your narrow views are oppressive," or "The Bible's been changed so many times," or "All religions are basically the same," they retreat in silence. They haven't been taught to simply raise their eyebrows and say, "Oh? How do you know?"

Critics rarely are prepared to defend their own "faith." They have seldom thought through what they believe and have relied more on generalizations and slogans than on careful reflection. To expose their error, take your cue from Lieutenant Columbo. Scratch your head, rub your chin, pause for a moment, then say, "Do you mind if I ask you a question?"

As with the emperor and his imaginary clothes, all it takes is one person to calmly say, "You're naked." That's the power of Columbo.

WHAT WE LEARNED IN THIS CHAPTER

In this chapter we focused on what happens *after* you have a conversation and are now looking back, trying to appraise your effectiveness as an ambassador. We started out by exploring three specific ways you can improve your skill at Columbo.

First, try to anticipate objections you might face, and then think of questions in advance. This allows you to formulate responses before the pressure is on. Second, take some time for self-assessment after each encounter. Ask how you could have phrased questions more effectively or conducted yourself differently in the conversation. Enlist a friend in the process, especially if he was with you during the dialogue. Finally, if you think of anything new, role-play your ideas — and potential rejoinders from the other side — out loud.

Next, we learned how to defend against the Columbo tactic when someone uses it against us. Remind yourself that you are in control of your side of the conversation. Politely refuse to answer the person's leading questions. Then, ask him to simply state his point and his reasons for it so you can give the issue some thought.

We also learned to be alert for questions that are not really questions at all, but assertions in disguise (e.g., "Who are you to say?"). When you encounter this situation, point out that the question is confusing. Then ask the person to rephrase it in the form of a statement. Or simply ask your first Columbo question, "What do you mean by that?"

PART TWO
FINDING
THE FLAWS

IT IS AXIOMATIC THAT THE MOST INTELLIGENT
PEOPLE — COLLEGE PROFESSORS, DOCTORS,
LAWYERS, PH.D.S, BRIGHT FOLKS OF ALL
STRIPES — MAKE FOOLISH AND ELEMENTARY
MISTAKES IN THINKING WHEN IT COMES TO
SPIRITUAL THINGS.

— Gregory Koukl

CHAPTER SEVEN

SUICIDE: VIEWS THAT SELF-DESTRUCT

SOMEONE once said that if you give a man enough rope, he'll hang himself. Our next tactic is based on the tendency of many erroneous views to self-destruct. Such ideas get caught in their own noose and quickly expire.

Commonly known as self-refuting views, these ideas defeat themselves. Like the sign in the restaurant saying, "Authentic Italian food served the traditional Chinese way," or the tabloid headline that reads, "Woman gives birth to her own father," views that commit suicide are often obvious.

Here is another example from a philosophy student's T-shirt. The front sported the caption, "The statement on the back of this shirt is false." The back of the shirt read, "The statement on the front of this shirt is true."

There is no need to expend energy addressing views that are bent on destroying themselves. They die by their own hand, saving you the trouble. If an atheist tells you he knows God doesn't exist because God told him so in a vision, your work is already done.[1] All you need to do is point out the problem and quietly watch the view commit hari-kari.

IF IT'S TRUE, IT'S FALSE

Every statement is about something. For example, the sentence "Cats chase rats" is about cats. Sometimes statements include themselves in what they refer to. The statement "All English sentences are false" is about all English sentences, including itself.

In this last case, you can immediately see a problem. The statement has within it the seeds of its own destruction. If all English sentences are false, then the English sentence declaring it so must also be false, and if false, then it is easily — and appropriately — dismissed. Because it cannot satisfy its own standard, it falls on its own sword.

When statements fail to meet their own criteria of validity, they are self-refuting. Even when they seem true at first glance (and many do), they still prove themselves false. The minute the words are uttered, they fail. Here are some conspicuous examples I have encountered over the years:

- "There is no truth." (Is this statement true?)
- "There are no absolutes." (Is this an absolute?)
- "No one can know any truth about religion." (And how, precisely, did you come to know that truth about religion?)
- "You can't know anything for sure." (Are you sure about that?)
- "Talking about God is meaningless." (What does this statement about God mean?)
- "You can only know truth through experience." (What experience taught you that truth?)
- "Never take anyone's advice on that issue." (Should I take your advice on that?)

The Suicide tactic works because of a rule of logic you are already familiar with, even if you don't know its name. It's called the law of noncontradiction. This law reflects the commonsense notion that contradictory statements cannot *both* be true at the same time.[2]

All suicidal views either express or entail contradictions. They make two different claims that are at odds with each other: "A" is the case and "A" is not the case. Obvious contradictions are often funny because we see the absurdity built into them:

- "I used to believe in reincarnation. But that was in a former life."[3] (I don't believe in reincarnation. I do believe in reincarnation.)
- "Nobody goes there anymore. It's too crowded." (It's not crowded. It is crowded.)
- "I wish I had an answer to that, because I'm tired of answering that question." (I don't know the answer to that question. I know the answer to that question.)
- "I really didn't say everything I said."[4] (I did not say it. I did say it.)
- "I never, never, repeat a word. Never." (I don't repeat a word. But I just did repeat a word.)
- "This page intentionally left blank." (This page is blank. This page is not blank.)
- "You're in rare form, as usual." (Your performance is rare. Your performance is not rare.)
- "These terrorists have technology we don't even know about." (We know about things we don't know about.)

When an idea or objection violates the law of noncontradiction in a straightforward fashion, I call it "Formal Suicide."

To recognize if a view has suicidal tendencies, first, pay attention to the basic idea, premise, conviction, or claim. Try to identify it. Next, ask if the claim applies to itself. If so, is there a conflict? Does the statement itself fail to live up to its own standards? Can it be stated in the form "A" is the case and "A" is not the case? If so, it commits suicide.

Here's another way of looking at it: *If exactly the same reasons in favor of another's view (or against your own) defeat the reasons themselves, then the view is self-defeating.*

The final step is easy. Simply point out the contradiction. For example, when someone says, "People should never impose their values on others," ask if those are *his* values (they are). Next ask why he's seeking to impose them on others. I have included more examples below so you can see precisely how this works.

It might have occurred to you that Columbo and Suicide work well together. If you notice that a person's viewpoint self-destructs, point it out with a question rather than a statement.

Arguments designed to show that a view is contradictory are always lethal if they can be sustained. The argument against God based on the existence of evil is popular precisely because it trades on a presumed contradiction. This gives it unstoppable force if it succeeds.[5] When a view commits suicide, it cannot be revived, because there is no way to repair it. Even God cannot give life to a contradictory notion.[6] Philosophers say such views are "necessarily false." They cannot be true in any possible way. Because they are dead on arrival, defending them is a lost cause.

You might wonder why anyone would believe self-refuting ideas. Very few people knowingly affirm contradictions (though some are so evident you wonder how they could be missed), but when contradictions are *implicit*, embedded in the larger idea, they are harder to see. This is why people are taken in by them.

For example, we know that the claim "My brother is an only child" is false because the concept of "brother" entails having a sibling. When Yogi Berra counsels, "Always go to other people's funerals, otherwise they won't go to yours," we chuckle. A person cannot pay his last respects at your funeral if he's dead.

Though these two contradictions are easy to spot, they are different from the explicit examples above. Here the contradictions are under the surface. Implicit contradictions are sometimes difficult to identify because they are hidden.

For the remainder of the chapter, I want to walk you through popular notions that are implicitly self-refuting. In each case, the problem is not immediately obvious. Each one fails, however, through contradiction. They are sunk before they ever set sail.

IS TRUTH TRUE?

I have already pointed out that the postmodern claim "There is no truth"[7] invites an obvious question: Is the claim that there is no truth *itself* a true statement, or is it false? If false, then false. If alleged true, then false again.

This fact became painfully obvious in my debate with philosopher Marv Meyer. I defended the resolve "Objective truth exists and can be known," while Dr. Meyer took the opposing side.

I want you to notice something about formal disputes like these. To debate, Dr. Meyer must argue against one view and in favor of another. This argument takes a very particular form: The view he opposes (mine) is false; the view he promotes (his) is true.

This is precisely what happened. With grace and considerable skill, the professor pointed out the failings of my perspective. Aristotle, it turns out, was wrong; Derrida was right. Mr. Koukl is mistaken; Marv Meyer is correct.

Do you see the problem here? Dr. Meyer marshaled an array of facts, truth, and knowledge for the purpose of persuading his audience that facts, truth, and knowledge are all sophisticated fictions.

In the course of the debate, I pointed this out to the audience. I mentioned that Dr. Meyer was forced by the nature of debate itself to make use of the very thing he was denying in the debate, dooming his effort to failure. Indeed, *merely by showing up*, Dr. Meyer had implicitly affirmed the resolve I was defending, effectively conceding the debate to me before it even began.

I further pointed out to the audience that every vote cast for Dr. Meyer as the winner of the debate meant the voter had been persuaded that Dr. Meyer's view was (objectively) true and mine was (objectively) false. Therefore, every vote for my opponent was really a vote for me.

The audience laughed, but the point wasn't lost on them. When the final tally came in, the good professor got only one vote (apparently someone wasn't listening). This wasn't because I was clever. It was because the view he was defending was obviously false, a fact that couldn't be missed once the problem was carefully pointed out.

The "Christian" version of postmodernism fares no better, even though baptized with religious language. This example from a Christian college was relayed to me by a student in the class.

"Are any of you in this room God?" The professor scanned the audience slowly, looking for takers. No hands went up.

"God knows 'TRUTH,'" she continued, writing the word in all capital letters on the board. "All truth is God's truth. God *is* truth. But you are not God. Therefore, you only know 'truth.'" She then scrawled in lower case this secondary and substandard take on reality next to the superior version that is forever out of reach for mere humans.

She paused for a moment, letting her point sink in, then closed. "Have a nice day," she said, and dismissed the class.

It was a brilliant piece of rhetorical wizardry. Students were too busy taking notes and worrying whether or not this would be on the test to think carefully about what had been stolen from them or the ruin this foreshadowed for their faith.

The professor's assertions teemed with confusion. What does "TRUTH" mean? Omniscience? That couldn't be her meaning. That God knows everything and we do not is a trivial observation, hardly a revelation even for college freshman.

Does she mean we can't know things *in the way* God knows them, that we don't see the world the way he does? Again, not particularly profound.

No, the professor was going after the conviction in "modernist" circles that human beings can actually know something like absolute truth — knowledge they can count on. Instead, she is saying that we mortals inhabit a kind of knowledge twilight where the outlines of reality are vague and indistinct, robbing us of all confidence that anything we think we know is actually so.

The professor seemed blind to her point's suicidal tendencies. The following questions make this failure obvious:

Professor, I'm confused about your comments. Is this insight you've offered true or false? I don't think you'd knowingly teach us something false, so you must think it true. And that's what confuses me. What kind of "truth" would that be? It couldn't be *TRUTH*, because you're not God. So it must be *truth*. But if this is just your personal perception of reality, why should any of us take you seriously? We have our own perceptions. Since none of us has *TRUTH*, who's to say who is right and who is wrong? Can you clear this up for me?

Paul warned us not to be taken "captive through philosophy and empty deception, according to the tradition of men, according to the elementary principles of the world, rather than according to Christ" (Colossians 2:8). Yet captivity abounds, even in places God intended to be a refuge from such error.

CAN GOD MAKE A ROCK SO BIG HE CAN'T LIFT IT?

This kind of challenge is called a "pseudo-question." It's like asking, "Can God win an arm wrestling match against himself?" or "If God beat himself up, who would win?" or "Can God's power defeat his own power?"

The question is nonsense because it treats God as if he were two instead of one. The comparative phrase "stronger than" can only be used when two subjects are in view, like when we say Bill is stronger than Bob, or my left arm is stronger than my right arm. Since God is only one, it makes no sense to ask if he is stronger than himself. The question proves nothing about any deficiency in God because the question itself — Can God's omnipotence defeat his omnipotence? — is incoherent.

"GOD DOESN'T TAKE SIDES."

This reprimand comes up every election cycle. In fact, I once saw a full-page ad in the *Los Angeles Times* lecturing one side of the political spectrum on this very point. The assertion is self-defeating, though, as illustrated in the following conversation:

"You think God is on your side, but you're wrong. God doesn't take sides."

"Let me ask you a question. In this disagreement we're having on whether or not God takes sides, what do you think God's opinion is?"

"I just told you. God is against taking sides."

"Right. So in our dispute, God would agree with you, not me."

"That's right."

"He would *side* with you in this issue, then. I guess God does take sides after all."

Note the contradiction: God does take sides. God doesn't take sides. The assertion was self-defeating. Not surprisingly, the ad went on to campaign for its own political view as the moral high ground, compounding the error.

TO ERR IS HUMAN

A common attack on the Bible goes like this: Men wrote the Bible. People are imperfect. Therefore, the Bible is flawed and not inspired by God.

Remember our rule for discovering suicidal statements: *If exactly the same reasons in favor of another's view (or against your own) defeat the reasons themselves, then the view is self-defeating.* The presumption that if man is *capable* of error, he *will* err also applies to this very argument against inspiration.

Consider this exchange:

"You think the Bible must be flawed because people make mistakes."

"Yes, that's the way it seems to me."

"I'm curious — why do you think you are an exception to that rule?"

"What do you mean?"

"Well, you don't seem to think you've made a mistake in your own judgment about the Bible. But you're a flawed human being, too."

"Of course I am. But I didn't mean that people always make mistakes."

"If people don't always make mistakes, though, you can't rule out the Bible just because people wrote it, can you?"

> It's not enough to dismiss the Bible simply by noting that "men wrote it." This, in itself, proves nothing. It doesn't follow that if people are **capable** of error, they always **will** err. Taken at face value, this objection is self-refuting.

C. S. Lewis cites a related example. In response to the Freudian and Marxist claim that all thoughts are tainted (either psychologically or ideologically) at their source, he writes:

If they say that all thoughts are thus tainted, then, of course, we must remind them that Freudianism and Marxism are as much systems of thought as Christian theology.... The Freudian and the Marxian are in the same boat with all the rest of us and cannot criticize us from the outside. They have sawn off the branch they are sitting on. If, on the other hand, they say that the taint need not invalidate their thinking, then neither need it invalidate ours. In which case they have saved their own branch, but also saved ours along with it.[8]

Statements like "Everyone's view is a product of his own prejudices" or "All your so-called 'facts' are only beliefs dictated by your cultural biases" falter for the same reason. Are these views themselves merely a product of prejudice or cultural bias? If so, why take them seriously?

"ATMAN IS BRAHMAN AND BRAHMAN IS ATMAN"

Hinduism as a religious view also seems compromised by contradictory notions. The pantheistic monism at the heart of this Eastern religion teaches that "reality" as we know it is an illusion — *maya* — of which each of us is part.

> If I am an illusion, how could I know it? How could I possess true knowledge that I do not exist? (I think, therefore I ain't?) Do people in a dream know they are imaginary? Does Charlie Brown know he is a cartoon character?

This Hindu concept that the world is an illusion contradicts the idea that I can know that I am a player in the illusion. Implicitly, it claims that I am not a real self and that I am a real self at the same time. Thus, this central doctrine of Hinduism self-destructs.

The most common escape route from this problem is the claim that the law of contradiction is a Western notion that doesn't apply in Eastern thought like Hinduism. Eastern thinkers are comfortable with contradiction, so they say.

This problem, though, has nothing to do with what people are "comfortable" with. It has to do with how reality is structured. People may be comfortable with all sorts of unusual things. This may tell you something about *psychology*, but not about *reality*.

Computers work on a binary system of 0s and 1s. The law of noncontradiction functions to keep these two distinct. It doesn't matter if the computer is in the Eastern Hemisphere or the Western Hemisphere or if the person at the keyboard is Christian, Hindu, Taoist, animist, or atheist. The computer works regardless because reality is still structured according to the law of non-contradiction, even if people from other cultures are psychologically confused about this point.

THEISTIC EVOLUTION: DESIGNED BY CHANCE?

Some people suggest that God used evolution to design the world. They are motivated, I think, by two impulses. The first is a desire to affirm the Bible. The second is a suspicion Darwinism might have merit. Thus, they declare both true.

These two notions, however, seem incompatible to me. It may sound reasonable for God to "use" evolution, but if you look closer I think you will see the problem.

Suppose I wanted a straight flush for a hand of poker. I could either pull the cards out of the deck individually and "design" the hand, or I could shuffle the cards randomly and see if the flush is dealt to me. It would not make any sense, though, to "design" the hand by shuffling the deck and dealing. There's no way to ensure the results. (I guess if I were really clever I could make it *look* like I was shuffling the deck when in reality I was stacking it, but that would be a deceitful kind of design called "cheating.")

In the same way, either God designs the details of the biological world, or nature shuffles the deck and natural selection chooses the winning hand. The mechanism is either conscious and intentional (design), or unconscious and unintentional (natural selection). Creation has a purpose, a goal. Evolution is accidental, like a straight flush dealt to a poker rookie.

The idea that something is designed by chance is contradictory. Like trying to put a square peg in a round hole, this just doesn't fit.

"ONLY SCIENCE GIVES RELIABLE TRUTH"

This modern slogan seems reasonable at first glance. Many people think knowledge begins and ends with the scientific method. Anything else is mere opinion and unsubstantiated belief, a view that is sometimes called "scientism." However, those who hold this view will be surprised to know that it commits suicide. Consider this dialog:

"I don't believe in religion."

"Why not?"

"There is no scientific evidence for it."

"Then you shouldn't believe in science either."

"Why not?"

"Because there is no scientific evidence for it."

This was a terse exchange, so let me expand a bit. I noticed first that the slogan "Only science gives reliable truth" is a statement *about* truth that also purports to *be* true, so it includes itself in what it refers to (in the same way that the statement "All English sentences are false" includes itself). Next, I simply applied our basic test for Suicide by asking, "Can the statement satisfy its own requirement?"

I quickly realized it could not. Since there is no scientific evidence proving that science is the only way to know truth, the view self-destructs. I then used Columbo to point out the flaw.[9]

The next time someone dismisses you with the "Only science gives reliable truth" canard, ask if he wants you to take his statement as fact or simply as unsubstantiated opinion. If fact, ask what testable scientific evidence led him to his conclusion. As it turns out, this claim is not a fact *of* science. It is a philosophical assertion *about* science that itself cannot be proven by the scientific method and would therefore be unreliable, according to this approach.

RELIGIOUS "SUICIDE"

The notion of religious pluralism, that all religions are equally true or valid, is also self-refuting. There are two different ways to demonstrate this.

First, if all religions are true, then Christianity is true. Yet a central claim of classical Christianity is that other religions are false when taken as a whole. Clearly, Jesus was not a pluralist. Either Christianity is correct that Jesus is God's Messiah for the world and other religions are deceptions, as Scripture teaches, or Christianity is false and some other view is true. In no case, though, can all religions be true and valid.

Second, when you think about it, religions have very diverse pictures of what the spiritual realm is like. Most forms of Hinduism teach that God is an impersonal force. Islam, Judaism, and Christianity teach that God is a personal being. In Buddhism, the question of God is irrelevant.

In classical theism, death is final, followed by either eternal reward or eternal punishment. In Eastern religions, death is a door the soul passes through many times as it works out its karma in reincarnation. Some religions teach that reprobates are destroyed while the righteous live on.

Can you see the problem? When someone dies, they *might* go to Heaven or Hell, or they *might* be reincarnated, or they *might* simply turn to dust, but *they can't do them all at the same time.*

Some religions are clearly mistaken on details central to their worldview. In fact, every one of them could be wrong on every single point, in principle, but they cannot all be right. Taken at face value, religious pluralism commits suicide.

YOU ARE WHAT YOU EAT?

I once saw a sign in a restaurant that read, "You are what you eat." I pointed out to the waitress that if we are what we eat, then we couldn't be something until we have eaten something. But we can't eat something unless we are something. Therefore, it's not true that we are what we eat.

The waitress, unschooled in the finer points of self-refuting arguments, looked at me and said, "You'll have to talk to the manager."

WHAT WE LEARNED IN THIS CHAPTER

First, we learned that we do not have to do all the work dealing with an argument or a challenge. Sometimes a view defeats itself. The tactic we use to expose this tendency is called Suicide.

Suicidal views have within them the seeds of their own destruction because they express contradictory concepts. They refute themselves. That's why they are called *self*-refuting.

Views that violate the law of noncontradiction are necessarily false. This means that nothing can be done to fix them. They are beyond repair in this world or *any* possible world. If a view entails contradiction — for example, "All English sentences are false" — there is no hope of reviving it. For this reason, the presence of contradiction is a decisive defeater of any argument or point of view.

We also learned how to recognize and respond to self-destructive statements. First, pay attention to the basic premise, conviction, or claim. Next, ask if the claim applies to itself. If so, does it satisfy its own criteria, or is there an internal contradiction? If the exact same reasons in favor of another's view (or against your own) defeat the reasons themselves, then the view is self-refuting. If you discover a problem, use a question (Columbo) rather than a statement to point it out.

Finally, we learned how to respond to popular examples of ideas or objections that violate the law of noncontradiction in a straightforward fashion (Formal Suicide). Remember, many formal contradictions are not immediately obvious. Instead, they are implicit, embedded in the larger idea. This makes them easy to miss. Even intelligent and educated people sometimes hold contradictory views without realizing it.

CHAPTER EIGHT

PRACTICAL SUICIDE

IN the last chapter, we learned that once in a while defending against an opposing view takes almost no work at all. Sometimes the easiest way to deal with another's objection is not to feed him more information, but rather to show him that his point commits suicide.

We have already explored the concept I called Formal Suicide, when an idea or objection violates the law of noncontradiction in a straightforward fashion. However, some views that are not internally contradictory can be self-defeating in other ways. "Practical Suicide," "Infanticide," and "Sibling Rivalry" are terms I use to describe three other ways statements or arguments self-destruct. I will take up Practical Suicide in this chapter, and discuss the other two in chapter 9.

PRACTICAL SUICIDE

Some points of view fail the pragmatic test. They simply cannot work in real-life application. There is no logical contradiction, strictly speaking, just a practical one. In this type of suicide, you can hold the view, but you can't promote it.

You see the conflict immediately in the claim, "It's wrong to say people are wrong." Holding that it is wrong to find fault with others is not itself incoherent. I know that sounds odd, considering the wording. But when you think about it, the problem occurs only when you *say* the statement. You would be doing the very thing you say should not be done. This kind of inconsistency is self-defeating because the person who voices this view contradicts his own convictions.

For example, like most two-year-olds, my little girl adopted a philosophy of "no" for a season. It was her answer to everything. I'd sometimes hear her alone playing in her room, absentmindedly stringing denials together with varying force and inflection, perfecting her technique like a piano virtuoso prepping for her next performance.

She was easy to trap, though. After a series of negatives I'd simply ask, "Are you going to answer 'no' again?" No matter what she answered, she'd be sunk. The philosophical subtlety was lost on her, but it should not escape you. There is no internal contradiction in a philosophy of "No." Once my daughter tried to practice her conviction consistently, though, she ran into trouble. This happens all the time, even with those old enough to know better.

> During a radio broadcast, I took exception to the theology of some televangelists. I was immediately challenged by a caller who said, "You shouldn't be correcting Christian teachers publicly on the radio."
>
> "Then why are you calling to correct me publicly on my radio show?" I asked.

Some people, convinced that arguing is prohibited by Scripture, argue tenaciously that I am being disobedient to biblical commands by taking contrary positions on the radio with my callers. Some reject the whole task of apologetics because they think reason is never adequate to discover truth. Then they painstakingly list the reasons they think their opinion is true (e.g., "I'll give you three good reasons why you can't use logic to find truth").

This is precisely the problem when people make the blanket statement that it is wrong to judge. Maybe it *is* wrong to make moral judgments, but using this rule to condemn a judgmental person is itself a breach of the principle.

When a caller to my radio show took me to task for condemning homosexuality, he soon found himself caught in his own net. The following conversation could be titled "Condemning Condemnation."

> *Lee:* I'm not a homosexual, but I think it's wrong to condemn anybody for anything.
>
> *Greg:* Why are you condemning me, then?
>
> *Lee:* What?
>
> *Greg:* I said, why are you condemning me if you think it's wrong to condemn people?
>
> *Lee:* I'm responding to the fact that a lot of Christians condemn people.
>
> *Greg:* I understand. And it sounds like you're condemning me because I just condemned homosexuality as wrong.
>
> *Lee:* Yes, I am. You are supposed to love everybody.
>
> *Greg:* Wait a minute. You're not listening to yourself. You just said it's wrong to condemn people. And now you admit you're condemning me. So I'm asking, why are you doing the very same thing that you say is wrong when I do it? *[Notice how I am narrating the argument here.]*
>
> *Lee:* No, I'm not. [Lee pauses as the light slowly begins to dawn.] Okay, let's put it this way. I'm not condemning you, I'm reprimanding you. Is that better?
>
> *Greg:* Then my comments about homosexuals are simple reprimands as well.[1]

I want you to notice two things about this exchange. First, it took Lee a few moments before he realized his error. This is not uncommon. Amazingly, some people never see it. When Lee finally came to his senses, his attempts at correcting his blunder were not helpful.

Second, since *I* saw the problem immediately, it wasn't difficult to come up with questions to press the issue from a number of different angles until Lee caught on.

> Philosopher Alvin Plantinga calls this suicidal tendency the "philosophical tar baby." If you get close enough to use the idea on someone else, he says, you're likely to get stuck fast to it yourself.[2]

MORAL RELATIVISM SELF-DESTRUCTS

Moral relativists — those who deny objective morality — are especially vulnerable to Practical Suicide. For example, whenever a relativist says, "You shouldn't force your morality on other people," I always ask, "Why not?"

What will he be able to say? He certainly can't respond by saying, "It's wrong." That option is no longer open to him. It is a contradiction, like saying, "There are no moral rules; here's one." This response commits suicide.

If a relativist does say it's wrong, I ask, "If you think it's wrong, then why are you doing it yourself? Why are you pushing your morality on me right now?"

The only consistent response for a relativist is, "Pushing morality is wrong *for me,* but that's just my personal opinion and has nothing to do with you. Please ignore me."

C. S. Lewis observes:

> Whenever you find a man who says he does not believe in a real Right and Wrong, you will find the same man going back on this a moment later. He may break his promise to you, but if you try breaking one to him he will be complaining "It's not fair".... A nation may say treaties do not matter; but then, next minute,

they spoil their case by saying that the particular treaty they want to break was an unfair one. But if ... there is no such thing as Right and Wrong ... what is the difference between a fair treaty and an unfair one?[3]

As I have written elsewhere, "A person can wax eloquent with you in a discussion on moral relativism, but he will complain when somebody cuts in front of him in line. He'll object to the unfair treatment he gets at work and denounce injustice in the legal system. He'll criticize crooked politicians who betray the public trust and condemn intolerant fundamentalists who force their moral views on others."[4]

I think this was Paul's point in Romans 2:1 when he wrote, "Therefore you are without excuse, every [one] of you who passes judgment, for in that you judge another, you condemn yourself; for you who judge practice the same things." Paul argued that those who set up their own morality are still faulted by their own code. Their "excuse" commits suicide.

> Usually a person cannot deny moral truth without immediately affirming it. The minute they say, "and it's wrong to push your morality on me," they have sunk their own ship.

TO RUSSIA, WITH LOVE

In 1976, a decade before the Iron Curtain came down, I spent five weeks with three others in a clandestine mission operation in Eastern Europe and the former Soviet Union. There I encountered a memorable example of Practical Suicide.

When we crossed the border from Romania into Moldavia, we were stopped on the Soviet side and searched. Once the border guards found Bibles, they took our car apart, checking everywhere for contraband. Then the questioning began. Where did we get the Bibles? Why were we bringing them across the border? Who were they for? Didn't we know such activity was illegal? It went on for hours.

We knew that the Soviets *claimed* they had religious freedom. They also *claimed* to print Bibles for their own people. We also knew that both claims were false, which gave us an advantage in the conversation.

"Don't you have freedom of religion in the Soviet Union?" we asked, parroting the propaganda.

"Yes, of course we have religious freedom," the interpreter shot back with some indignation, "but we have separation of church and state."

Now, it wasn't clear to us how bringing Bibles across the border actually interfered with that principle. Yet it was the interpreter's stock reply to just about every objection we raised.

"It is forbidden to bring Bibles and other religious material into the Soviet Union," she continued. "In schools we teach the children that there is no God. Only old people believe that. Our people are taught Marxist-Leninism. We don't allow any other propaganda. We have separation of church and state."

"But you print Bibles in the Soviet Union, right?" I asked.

"Yes, we do," she answered. "Our believers get all the Bibles they need."

"And you have religious freedom?"

"Yes, we have religious freedom, but we have separation of church and state."

"But we can't bring Bibles across the border?"

"No, we don't allow that propaganda in our country."

"The Bible is propaganda?"

"Yes."

"But you print Bibles in your own country."

"Yes."

"Now I'm confused," I remarked. "You say you have religious freedom, but we are not allowed to bring Bibles into your country because they are propaganda. Then you tell me you print Bibles in the Soviet Union."

She nodded in agreement to each point. I was surprised she couldn't see what was coming. "Then apparently your government is printing anti-communist propaganda right in your own country."

"No, you don't understand," she replied. "We have separation of church and state."

PROSELYTIZING PROHIBITED

Some years ago, the Southern Baptist Convention publicized its plans to direct its annual summer evangelistic outreach to Jews living in Chicago. It then encouraged Baptists to "pray each day for Jewish individuals you know by name that they will find the spiritual wholeness available through the Messiah."

The public reaction was immediate and severe. The director of the Jewish Anti-Defamation League said the campaign "projects a message of spiritual narrowness that invites theological hatred."[5] A consortium of religious groups in Chicago, including Christian denominations, issued a statement condemning the SBC, warning that the Baptists' evangelism in the Windy City would encourage hate crimes.

The grievances were aired on a national TV talk show, where two enraged rabbis from New York and Chicago confronted two Baptists. The substance of their complaint was this: Proselytizing should be reserved for people with no spiritual convictions. Jews already have a religion. It's the height of arrogance to suggest that they need a new one. Therefore, Christians should make their appeal elsewhere. Essentially, the rabbis were saying, "Keep your spiritual opinions to yourself. Stop trying to change other people's religious views."

Do you see the problem here? The rabbis were incensed that Christians were trying to change the religious convictions of Jews. Yet their antidote was for the Christians to abandon their own religious view of evangelism and adopt the rabbis' view.

In the heat of the moment, it probably did not occur to the Christians to simply ask, "If that's what you believe, then I don't understand why *you* are trying to change *my* religious beliefs right now. Why do you interfere when I'm trying to obey Jesus' command to preach the gospel? Why don't you keep your *own* religious views to yourself?"

Oddly, the Baptists were branded intolerant merely for planning to engage others in voluntary, thoughtful conversation about religion. Yet the rabbis who viciously condemned them on national television were considered "tolerant" and "open-minded."

The claim "It's wrong to try to change other people's religious beliefs" is usually an example of Practical Suicide. The idea itself is not incoherent. However, a person risks contradiction simply by trying to promote this conviction.

FREEDOM, REASON, AND KNOWLEDGE

It always strikes me as odd when people try to advance arguments for determinism. Let me tell you why.

Determinists claim that freedom is an illusion. Each of our choices is fixed, determined beforehand by the circumstances that precede it. All of our "choices" are inevitable results of blind physical forces beyond our control.

The problem with this view is that without freedom, rationality would have no room to operate. Arguments would not matter, since no one would be able to base beliefs on adequate reasons. One could never judge between a good idea and a bad one. One would only hold beliefs because he had been predetermined to do so.

That's why it is odd when someone tries to *argue* for determinism. If determinism were true, the person would have been "determined" to believe in it (with others just as "determined" to disagree). He would have to admit that reasons don't matter and that trying to think the issue through is a waste of time.

Although it is theoretically possible that determinism is true — there is no internal contradiction, as far as I can tell — no one could ever *know* it if it were. Every one of our thoughts, dispositions, and opinions would have been decided for us by factors completely out of our control. Therefore, in practice, arguments for determinism are self-defeating.

WHAT WE LEARNED IN THIS CHAPTER

In this chapter we discovered that there is more than one way for an argument to self-destruct. Though some views are not internally contradictory — that is, they do not fail through Formal Suicide — still, in practice they are self-defeating. The view can be believed, but not acted on or promoted. Anyone advancing the opinion cannot avoid violating his own convictions, for example, "It's wrong to say people are wrong."

We call this tendency "Practical Suicide." Moral relativists are especially vulnerable to this problem, as are those who believe it is wrong to try to change another person's religious views.

CHAPTER NINE

SIBLING RIVALRY AND INFANTICIDE

ARGUMENTS or points of view can self-destruct for a variety of different reasons. We have already talked about two: Formal Suicide and Practical Suicide. Now I would like to introduce you to a couple more that are not internally contradictory, but are self-defeating in their own unique ways.

Sometimes a conflict arises when a person raises two objections that are at odds with each other. This "Sibling Rivalry" is easy to spot if you look for it. At other times, someone's view is built on a prior concept that turns out to disqualify the view itself. I call this "Infanticide." Think of it like a deranged creature from a sci-fi movie that devours its own offspring. This kind of Suicide is more difficult to spot, but it is a powerful defeater nonetheless. In either case, the hard work is already done for you.

SIBLING RIVALRY

Occasionally in conversations you will notice something odd. You will hear a pair of objections voiced by the same person, but the complaints are logically inconsistent with each other. They are like children fighting between themselves, siblings in rivalry.

Since both objections cannot be simultaneously legitimate, your task is cut in half. A fair-minded person will surrender at least one when you identify the problem. Graciously point out the conflict, then ask which is the real concern. Sometimes this move effectively silences both objections because the person you are talking with realizes she has been unreasonable.

Is Gandhi in Heaven?

When I was in India, Christian apologist Prakesh Yesudian told me of a conversation he had with a Hindu about Gandhi, who is much revered there. Notice how Prakesh coupled Columbo with the Sibling Rivalry tactic.

"Is Gandhi in Heaven?" the Hindu asked. "Heaven would be a very poor place without Gandhi in it."

"Well, sir," Prakesh answered, "you must at least believe in Heaven then. And apparently you have done some thinking about what would qualify someone for Heaven. Tell me, what kind of people go to Heaven?"

"Good people go to Heaven," he responded.

"But this idea of what is a good person is very unclear to me. What is good?"

In typical Hindu fashion he replied, "Good and bad are relative. There is no clear definition."

"If that is true, sir, that goodness is relative and can't be defined, how is it you assume Gandhi is good and should be in Heaven?"

Either Gandhi fulfills some external standard of goodness, thus qualifying for Heaven, or goodness is relative and therefore a meaningless term when applied to anyone, including Gandhi. Both cannot be true at the same time.

Kavita

During that same trip, I had a discussion with a Hindu college student named Kavita. As I talked about Christianity, she raised the standard objection. "If God is as you say, how could he allow such suffering, especially for the children?" She gestured with a sweep of her hand as if to take in the collective anguish of Madras, which was great.

The first thing I pointed out was that God hadn't done this to India. Hinduism had. Ideas have consequences, and the suffering in Madras was a direct result of things Hindus believe.

I then explained that it wouldn't always be this way. A day would come when all evil would be destroyed, and Jesus himself would wipe away every bitter tear.

"How could that be?" she objected. "Evil and good exist as dual poles. If you have no evil, it is impossible to have good. Each must balance the other out."

I noticed immediately that Kavita's response was at odds with her first question. "Let me repeat this reasoning back to you," I said, "and you tell me what you think of it." She nodded.

"You ask 'Why are innocent children starving in the streets?' I answer, 'Good and evil exist as dual poles. Children starve in Madras so kids in other parts of the world may be happy and well. The one balances the other out.' What do you think?"

When the point sunk in, she was forced to smile. "Touché!" she replied.

"The Quarrel"

I encountered a clear example of Sibling Rivalry after an airing of *The Quarrel*, a film that explored the problem of God and the Holocaust. Director David Brandes had asked me to help moderate a discussion with an audience about the moral issues raised by the film.

From one side of the auditorium a Jewish woman offered that maybe God allowed the Holocaust as a punishment for Israel's wayward drift into secularism. Some Jewish thinkers have raised this possibility in light of the promised curses of Deuteronomy 28. The reflection prompted a sarcastic, "Well, that's a real loving God," from the other side of the theater.

I called attention to the conflict suggested by the second comment. Those who are quick to object that God isn't doing enough about evil in the world ("A good God wouldn't let that happen") are often equally quick to complain when God puts his foot down ("A loving God would never send anyone to Hell").

If God appears indifferent to wickedness, his goodness is challenged. Yet if he acts to punish sin, his love is in question. These objections compete with each other in most cases. They are siblings in rivalry. One or the other needs to be surrendered. Both can't be held simultaneously.[1]

Who Are You to Say?

Sibling Rivalry is the type of Suicide moral relativists commit when they object to the problem of evil. This happened at a restaurant during a conversation with a waitress (I seem to get in a lot of discussions with waitresses).

At first the young lady talked like a relativist: Everyone has his own morality. Right and wrong is a private affair. Who's to judge? As our conversation ranged over other topics, though, the problem of evil came up. How could God exist when there is so much evil in the world?

I want you to notice something about the problem of evil. The entire objection hinges on the observation that evil exists "out there" as an objective feature of the world. That is a serious problem for relativists, though.

According to relativism, when someone uses the word "evil," he is expressing a personal preference. The sentence "Premarital sex is wrong" means nothing more than "I don't prefer sex outside of marriage," or "Extramarital sex is wrong *for me*." Strictly speaking, the person is not talking about sex at all. The relativist is talking about himself.

In that light, imagine how silly this conversation would sound:

"I can't believe in God."

"Why not?"

"Brussels sprouts."

"Brussels sprouts? What do Brussels sprouts have to do with anything?"

"Did you ever taste those things? They're awful."

"I agree with you about Brussels sprouts, but some people do like them. What does the fact that you don't like Brussels sprouts have to do with God's existence?

"I can't believe in a God who would create something that tastes so awful to me."

This kind of objection is trivial. If relativism were true, talk of evil as an objection to God's existence would be nonsense. The complaint would mean nothing more than, "If God were really good, he wouldn't allow things that I don't like."

C. S. Lewis summed it up this way:

> Of course, I could have given up my idea of justice by saying it was nothing but a private idea of my own [relativism]. But if I did that, then my argument against God collapsed too — for the argument depended on saying that the world was really unjust, not simply that it did not happen to please my private fancies.[2]

To say that something is evil is to say it is not the way it is supposed to be. This makes no sense unless things are *supposed to be* different. Yet this is precisely what the relativist denies.

This waitress promoted two rival concepts at the same time — *subjective* morality and *objective* evil. The objections compete with each other. They were siblings in rivalry. G. K. Chesterton saw the problem over half a century ago:

> [The modernist] goes first to a political meeting where he complains that savages are treated as if they were beasts. Then he takes his hat and umbrella and goes on to a scientific meeting where he proves that they practically are beasts.... In his book on politics he attacks men for trampling on morality, and in his book on ethics he attacks morality for trampling on men.[3]

The belief that objective good and evil do not exist (relativism) is in conflict (rivalry) with a rejection of God based on the existence of objective evil.

Just Doin' What Comes Naturally

If homosexuality is morally neutral because it's natural, then adoption by same-sex couples must be wrong because for homosexuals, parenthood would be unnatural. The same principle governs both issues. If nature dictates morality,[4] and the natural consequence for homosexuals is to be childless, then it's unnatural — and therefore immoral — for homosexuals to raise children.

Artificial insemination of lesbians or adoptions by same-sex couples would be wrong by the logic of their own argument. This is a Sibling Rivalry suicide.

INFANTICIDE

I have saved Infanticide suicide for last because it is the most difficult to understand. Let me start with an example. Think for a moment about how this simpleminded father closed a letter to his son in college: "Son, if you didn't get this letter, please let me know, and I'll send another. I made a copy."

This makes us chuckle for a reason. The son would have to receive the letter in order to ask for a copy, but then he wouldn't need it. If he never got the original, he wouldn't know to ask for a replacement. There is a certain dependency relationship in play here that is at the heart of Infanticide.

Sometimes an objection (the "child") is dependent on a prior notion (the "parent") that must be in place for the challenge to be offered. For example, saying, "Vocal chords do not exist" is not internally contradictory. But since it requires vocal chords to *say* it, making the statement results in contradiction. The parent concept (vocal chords) devours the child (the claim there are no vocal chords). That's why I call this variation "Infanticide" suicide.

If a claim cannot be made unless the parent concept on which it depends is true, yet the claim denies the parent concept, then the argument commits Infanticide. The child is destroyed by the parent it relies on.

Bowling and Badness

The most powerful example of Infanticide that I know of has to do with the problem of evil. We looked at one complaint by *relativists* related to evil that was compromised due to Sibling Rivalry. When *objectivists* argue that God cannot exist because of evil, however, their view fails in a different way. It commits Infanticide.

> Surprisingly, instead of evil being a good argument **against** God, I am convinced it is one of the best evidences **for** God.

The first question the atheist must answer is, "What do you mean by 'evil'?" His impulse will be to give *examples* of evil (murder, torture, oppression, etc.). But that misses the point. Why call those things evil to begin with? One must first know *what* evil is before one can point to *examples* of it.

I want you to think about the concepts of "good" and "bad" for a moment. How do you know the difference between, for example, a good bowler and a bad one? Only one thing matters in bowling. The person who knocks down the most pins wins. It's the score that counts.

Knowing the difference between mediocre and masterful in anything requires a way of keeping score. There must be some standard of perfection by which to measure a performance. In bowling that standard is 300 — every pin down in every frame (some people have done this). If you are a golfer, one stroke per hole — a hole-in-one with every swing — is golfing perfection (no one has ever done this).

Notice that even when perfection is not attainable (a golf score of 18 on an 18-hole course), a scoring system is still necessary to differentiate between excellence, mediocrity, and abject failure. In the same way, moral judgments require a way of keeping score to distinguish virtue from vice.

Earlier in the chapter I observed that we use the word "evil" when we see things that are not the way they are supposed to be. We have a standard in mind—a moral scoring system of sorts—that allows us to recognize moral shortfalls. The reason we say some things are evil is we realize that they score low on the goodness scale. If there were no standard, there could be no error. C. S. Lewis notes:

> My argument against God was that the universe seemed so cruel and unjust. But how had I gotten this idea of just and unjust? A man does not call something crooked unless he has some idea of a straight line.[5]

This is precisely the problem for the atheist. He must answer the question: Where does the moral scoring system come from that allows one to identify evil in the first place? Where is the transcendent standard of objective good that makes the whole notion of evil intelligible? Are moral laws the product of chance? If so, why obey them? What—or who—establishes how things are supposed to be?

A moral rule is a command. Commands are features of minds. Ethicist Richard Taylor explains: "A duty is something that is owed … but something can be owed only to some person or persons. There can be no such thing as a duty in isolation.… The concept of moral obligation [is] unintelligible apart from the idea of God. The words remain, but their meaning is gone."[6]

There seems to be no good way to account for a transcendent standard of objective good—the moral rules that are violated by people who commit the evil in question—without the existence of a transcendent moral rule maker. In the movie *The Quarrel*, Rabbi Hersh challenges the secularist Chaim on this very point:

> If there's nothing in the universe that's higher than human beings, then what's morality? Well, it's a matter of opinion. I like milk; you like meat. Hitler likes to kill people; I like to save them. Who's to say which is better? Do you begin to see the horror of this? If there is no Master of the universe, then who's to say that

Hitler did anything wrong? If there is no God, then the people that murdered your wife and kids did nothing wrong.[7]

A morally perfect God is the only adequate standard for the system of scoring that makes sense of the existence of evil to begin with. Since God must exist to make evil intelligible, evil cannot be evidence against God. The complaint commits Infanticide.[8]

> Ironically, evil does not prove atheism. It proves just the opposite. There can only be a problem of evil **if** God exists. It is a problem only a **theist** can raise, not an **atheist**. When an atheist voices the concern, he gets caught in a suicidal dilemma.[9]

Notice that this difficulty is a little different from the Sibling Rivalry problem with evil mentioned earlier. In that case, two incompatible contentions rested *side by side*: The first is that true evil *does not* exist because morality is relative; the second is that evil *does* exist, so God's existence is in question. When someone simultaneously holds that evil does and does not exist, there is an irreconcilable conflict—a sibling rivalry. One or the other has to go.

With Infanticide, however, the notion of morality (with its corresponding concept of evil) *rests upon* the prior foundation of God's existence. God's existence seems to be necessary in order for any conversation about evil to be coherent. Thus, it can never be used to refute God, because without God the objection would have no meaning.

Moral Atheists?

Christians who grasp that God is necessary for morality sometimes make a blunder. They mistakenly conclude that atheists cannot be moral. Michael Shermer, atheist editor of *Skeptic* magazine, fires back, "Look, I'm an atheist, and I'm moral."

Both the criticism and the response miss the point. The question is not whether an atheist can *be* moral, but whether he can *make sense of* morality in a universe without God. Gravity still works even when people have no explanation for why it works.

The "why it works" question is what philosophers call the grounding problem. What grounds morality? What does it stand on, so to speak? What explanation best accounts for a moral universe? What worldview makes the most sense out of the existence of evil *or* good?

Atheism is a physicalist system that does not have the resources to explain a universe thick with nonphysical things like moral obligations. Neither can Eastern religion, by the way. If reality is an illusion, as classical Hinduism holds, then the distinction between good and evil is meaningless.

Someone like the Judeo-Christian God must exist in order to adequately account for moral laws. Theism solves the grounding problem for morality. This explains how even an atheist like Michael Shermer is capable of noble conduct: He still lives in God's world.

More Scientific Suicide

I want to revisit a problem that came up earlier. In chapter 7 I showed how the idea that science is the only source of reliable truth committed what I called Formal Suicide. However, this notion is doubly dead because it commits Infanticide, too.

The term "scientism" describes the view that science is the only reliable method of knowing truth about the world. Accordingly, "Everything outside of science is a matter of mere belief and subjective opinion," says J. P. Moreland, "of which rational assessment is impossible."[10]

Here is how scientism self-destructs. Imagine you wanted to collect all knowledge in a box. Let's call it the "Truth Box." Before any alleged truth could go into the box, it must first pass the scientific truth test (the claim of scientism).

The problem is that your knowledge project could never get started because some truths need to be in the Truth Box first before science itself could begin its analysis. The truths of logic and mathematics must be in the box, for example, along with the truth of the basic reliability of our senses. Certain moral truths — like "Report all data honestly" — must be in the box. In fact, the entire scientific method must be in the box before the method itself can be used to test the truthfulness of anything else.

None of these truths can be established by the methods of science, because science cannot operate in a knowledge vacuum. Certain truths — known through means other than science — must be in place before science can begin testing for other truths. Since the notion of scientism (the child) is inconsistent with the presuppositions that make science possible (the parent), scientism as a comprehensive view of knowledge commits Infanticide.

THE TACTICAL GOAL OF SUICIDE

When I use any form of the Suicide tactic, I have a specific goal in mind. I want to show the person that there is a fatal inconsistency in his beliefs. This is a problem I think he would correct if he really understood it. Furthermore, the contradiction suggests that deep down he does not really believe everything he has said.

For example, when he says "There is no truth," he actually believes there are some truths, but is doubtful about others (probably the one you are talking with him about). When he says, "It's wrong for you to push your morality on others," it's clear he doesn't think this is always wrong, only sometimes (probably in your case).

I think you can see how the Suicide tactic is not an end in itself, but can be used as a bridge to further questions. What kind of evidence is adequate to give us confidence that something is true? Under what circumstances might we legitimately impose our morality on someone else? Do those circumstances apply here?

WHAT WE LEARNED IN THIS CHAPTER

We finished our look at the Suicide tactic by considering two final ways that views self-destruct: Sibling Rivalry and Infanticide.

Sometimes objections come in pairs that are logically inconsistent with each other. Like children fighting, they are in opposition, siblings in rivalry. Since they contradict each other, both objections could not be legitimate complaints. At least one can be eliminated by pointing out the conflict.

Infanticide is a little more difficult to grasp. Sometimes an objection (the "child") is dependent on a prior notion (the "parent") that must be in place for the challenge to be offered. If a claim cannot be made unless the parent concept on which it depends is true, yet the claim denies the parent concept, then the parent kills the child, and the argument commits Infanticide.

We saw how this type of Suicide applied to the problem of evil. Since God's existence is necessary to make the notion of evil intelligible, the existence of evil cannot be used as a proof that God does not exist. It proves just the opposite. Simply put, if evil exists, then good exists. If good exists, then God exists. Ironically, the existence of evil is powerful evidence *for* God, not *against* him.

CHAPTER 10

TAKING THE ROOF OFF

SOME points of view, if taken seriously, don't actually commit suicide, but they work against themselves in a different way. When played out consistently, they lead to unusual — even absurd — conclusions.

To understand how this works, you might think of maps and highways. If you were visiting Los Angeles and wanted to go to Santa Barbara up the coast, someone might draw a map to guide you to your destination. If, however, you followed the instructions very carefully and took the highway they suggested, but found yourself in Riverside on your way to the desert, you would know something was wrong with the route you were given.

In a similar fashion, worldviews are like maps. They are someone's idea of what the world is like. The individual ideas making up a worldview are like highways leading to different destinations. If you use the map but arrive at a strange destination, either part of the map is inaccurate (the part about the highway you were driving on), or the map itself is the wrong one for the region.

I realize that this last option is not likely when you are talking about real maps. I doubt if you would try to find your way around New York using a map of Chicago. But this kind of thing happens all the time with worldviews. Sometimes the roads are wrong on otherwise good worldview maps. At other times, worldview maps are completely inadequate for the actual terrain.

Keep this illustration in mind as we explore our next tactic. It is a method that helps you determine the accuracy of someone's map of reality—their worldview—by noting where the route on the map leads them.

> If you help someone see in advance that the route his map recommends will actually lead him off a cliff, he might consider changing his course. He might even discover he is using the wrong worldview map altogether and exchange it for one that is more reliable.

TAKING A TEST DRIVE

I first learned the tactic of Taking the Roof Off from Francis Schaeffer. The tactic itself is simple. First, adopt the other person's viewpoint for the sake of argument. Next, give his idea a test drive. Try to determine where you will end up if you follow his instructions faithfully. If you arrive at an odd destination, point it out and invite the person to reconsider his starting point.

Sometimes when you press an idea to its logical consequences, the result is counterintuitive or absurd. If you take a view seriously and apply it consistently and it leads to disaster, you are on the wrong route. Something must be wrong with where you started if this is the place you end up.

This tactic makes it clear that certain arguments prove too much. It forces people to ask if they can really live with the kind of world they are affirming. Those who are intellectually honest will think twice about embracing a view that ultimately leads to irrationality, incoherence, and absurdity. That is too high a price to pay.

Taking the Roof Off is also known as *reductio ad absurdum* (or simply *reductio*). This is a Latin phrase that means to reduce a point to its absurd conclusion or consequence.

WHY REDUCTIOS WORK

When I was a young Christian, I read Francis Schaeffer's *The God Who Is There*. Schaeffer argues that Christians have a powerful ally in the war of ideas: reality. Whenever someone tries to deny the truth, reality ultimately betrays him. As Schaeffer points out, "Regardless of a man's system, he has to live in God's world."[1]

The fact is, mankind is made in the image of God and must live in the world God created. Although culture shifts, human nature remains the same. Ideas change, but ultimate reality does not.

> Every person who rejects the truth of "the God who is there" is caught between the way he **says** the world is and the way the world **actually** is.

This dissonance, what Schaeffer called the "point of tension," is what makes Taking the Roof Off so effective. Any person who denies the truth of God's world lives in contradiction. On the surface he claims one thing, yet deep inside he believes something else because he knows the truth. To protect himself from considering the consequences of this conflict, he subconsciously erects a defense, a deceptive cover, a "roof." Simply put, he's in denial. Our job is to remove that roof, expose the fraud, and deprive him of his false sense of security. In Schaeffer's words:

Every man has built a roof over his head to shield himself at the point of tension.... The Christian, lovingly, must remove the shelter [the roof] and allow the truth of the external world and of what man is to beat upon him. When the roof is off, each man must stand naked and wounded before the truth of what is.... He must come to know that his roof is a false protection from the storm of what is.[2]

Regardless of our ideological impulses, deep inside each of us is a commonsense realist. Those who are not realists are either dead, in an institution, or sleeping in cardboard boxes under the freeway.

Knowing this gives us a tremendous advantage. The key to dealing with moral relativism, for example, is realizing that for all the adamant affirmations, no one really believes it, and for a good reason: If you start with relativism, reality does not make sense.

It is significant that those who want to practice relativism never want relativism practiced *toward them*. For example, Schaeffer tells of an encounter with a Hindu student at Cambridge who had been vigorously condemning Christianity.

"Am I not correct in saying," Schaeffer asked, "that on the basis of your system, cruelty and noncruelty are ultimately equal, that there is no intrinsic difference between them?" The Hindu nodded. To his alarm, a student who understood the implications of this view took a kettle of boiling water and held it above the Hindu's head repeating, "There is no difference between cruelty and non-cruelty."[3] The Hindu turned on his heel and walked out.

When I lectured on relativism at UC Berkeley, I asked a question I pose frequently at secular universities: Why do we all feel guilty?

"Maybe guilt is just a cultural construction," I offered. "I guess that's possible. But there's another possibility. Maybe you *feel* guilty ... because you *are* guilty."

I have asked this question countless times on campuses. No one has ever stopped me afterward and said I was wrong — that they did *not* feel guilty. They could not. They knew better. Which makes my closing statement to the audience all the more powerful. "The answer to guilt is not denial," I say. "The answer to guilt is forgiveness. And this is where Jesus comes in."

My question at Berkeley was a direct application of Schaeffer's insight. We start with the truth of the world as each person already knows it to be. Then we offer an explanation that resonates with her deepest intuitions and makes sense of the reality she encounters every day.

We start with guilt, then reason back to morality and a moral lawgiver. We start with evidence for design, then reason back to a designer. We start with personal worth and significance, then reason backward to the source of all meaning. We start with reality, then reason backward to a cause that makes the best sense of what people already know to be true.

In a very real sense, every person who denies God is living on borrowed capital. He enjoys living as if the world is filled with morality, meaning, order, and beauty, yet he denies the God whose existence makes such things possible.

> When you start with theism — "In the beginning, God" — these destinations make complete sense. When you start with materialism, though — "In the beginning, the particles" — that route takes you over a cliff of absurdity and despair.

ROOF REMOVAL, STEP BY STEP

Taking the Roof Off is not complicated if you follow these three steps. First, reduce the person's point of view to its basic argument, assertion, principle, or moral rule. This might take a moment of reflection. Ask yourself what the person's *specific* claim is. The first step of Columbo is handy at this point. State the idea clearly (write it out if you need to). If this is part of a conversation, check with the person to make sure you got it right. You might say, "Let me see if I understand you correctly," then repeat the point as clearly as you can.

Second, mentally give the idea a "test drive" to see where it leads. Ask: "If I follow this principle consistently, what implications will it have for other issues? Will it produce a 'truth' that seems wrong or counterintuitive? Will any absurd consequences result?" The answer to these questions sometimes occurs later, after you have given the issue more thought.

Third, if you find a problem, point it out. Invite the other person to consider the implications of her view and the absurd end that follows from it. Show her that if she applies her view consistently, it will take her to a destination that seems unreasonable. Therefore, something about her original view needs to be modified.

For example, Mother Theresa once appealed to the governor of California to stay the execution of double murderer Robert Alton Harris. Her reasoning: Since "Jesus would forgive," the governor should forgive.

This argument proves too much, as our tactic demonstrates. When applied consistently, it becomes a reason to forgo any punishment for any crime because one could always argue, "Jesus would forgive." Emptying every prison does not seem to be what Jesus had in mind because great evil would result. Capital punishment might be faulted on other grounds, but not on this one. Here is the analysis:

> **Claim**: If Jesus would forgive capital criminals, then it is wrong to execute them.
>
> **Taking the Roof Off**: On this reasoning, it would be wrong for government to punish *any* criminals because one could always say, "Jesus would forgive." This seems absurd, especially when Scripture states that the purpose of government is to punish evildoers, not forgive them.[4]
>
> **Therefore**: Even though *Jesus* might forgive murderers, that does not mean it is wrong for the *government* to punish them.

Here's another example. Typically, social conservatives in this country think it is wrong for the government to endorse same-sex relationships by granting them marriage licenses. A common rejoinder is, "That's the same thing people said about interracial marriages." The assumption with this remark is that since people were wrong then, they must be wrong now.

To Take the Roof Off, first ask what the core argument is. In this case, it's a little tricky, but I think this sums it up: We were wrong in the *past* on *one* issue (interracial marriage). Therefore, we are wrong in the *present* on a *different* issue (same-sex marriage). The following dialogue demonstrates how absurd this logic is:

"I don't think same-sex unions should be endorsed by the government."

"You know, people said the very same thing about interracial marriages. They were wrong then, and you are wrong now. Same-sex marriage is right."

"So you think the government should *approve* of homosexual unions?"

"Of course."

"But people said the government should approve *slavery*, too. They were wrong then, and you are wrong now. Same-sex marriage is wrong."

Here's the breakdown:

Claim: Argument: Because people were wrong in the past on one issue, they are wrong in the present on a different issue.

Taking the Roof Off: Since the government was wrong endorsing slavery in the past, it would be wrong for them to endorse same-sex marriage in the present. This is absurd because the same kind of reasoning produces contradictory results: Same-sex marriage is wrong, *and* same-sex marriage is right (see above).

Therefore: It is not sound to argue that just because people were wrong in the past about interracial marriage, they are now wrong about same-sex marriage.

The only way out of this problem is to show a similarity between interracial marriage and same-sex marriage that is relevant to the issue of government endorsement. There is none.

Jesus used the Taking the Roof Off tactic in an argument with the Pharisees. Notice how He reduced the Pharisees' reasoning to its logical and absurd conclusion:

But when the Pharisees heard it, they said, "This man casts out demons only by Beelzebul the ruler of the demons." And knowing their thoughts He said to them, "Any kingdom divided against itself is laid waste; and any city or house divided against itself shall not stand. And if Satan casts out Satan, he is divided against himself; how then shall his kingdom stand?... But if I cast out demons by the Spirit of God, then the kingdom of God has come upon you" (Matthew 12:24–26, 28).

Here's how the tactic played out:

Claim: Jesus casts out demons by the power of Satan.

Taking the Roof Off: If Satan is the source of Jesus' power, then Satan is casting out Satan, destroying his own kingdom. This is absurd.

Therefore: Jesus' power must not come from Satan, but from God who opposes Satan. Those who oppose Jesus, then, are not opposing Satan, but God.

Each vignette below tackles a common challenge using Taking the Roof Off. Notice how many ways this technique can be used. It is flexible because people frequently hold beliefs that lead to absurd consequences.

BORN BAD?

It's common of late to justify one's sexual "orientation" by an appeal to nature. Some people think the claim "I was born this way" is all that's needed to stem moral criticism of homosexuality. But why settle for this approach? Why think the state of nature is an appropriate guide to morality?

The basic argument can be summed up this way: Anything that is natural is also moral. Homosexuality is natural (the claim goes). Therefore, homosexuality is moral. What happens when we go down that road?

I once asked a radio caller who used this reasoning if the same rationale would justify gay-bashing. If scientists isolated a gay-bashing gene, would violence toward homosexuals be acceptable? Hardly. If there really were a gay-bashing gene, the correct response would be to fight its influence, not to surrender to it.

Seventeenth-century philosopher Thomas Hobbes noted famously that life in an unregulated state of nature is "solitary, poor, nasty, brutish, and short." Morality protects us from the brutality of living in a world where people act out their impulses. *Animals* always do what comes naturally.

Since living according to nature would result in all kinds of barbarism, how does it make sense to invoke the natural state of things to justify anything? The difference between doing what comes naturally and principled self-restraint is called civilization. Morality that counters one's natural inclinations rather than approves them is our only refuge from a life that is "solitary, poor, nasty, brutish, and short."

Here's how the reductio looks:

Claim: Any "natural" tendency or behavior is morally acceptable.

Taking the Roof Off: If gay-bashing comes naturally for someone, it must be okay. This is obviously wrong.

Therefore: Just because an impulse is natural does not mean it's moral. Homosexuality cannot be justified this way.

CHALK ONE UP FOR GOD

The story is told of an atheist philosophy professor who performed a parlor trick each term to convince his students that there is no God.[5] "Anyone who believes in God is a fool," he said. "If God existed, he could stop this piece of chalk from hitting the ground and breaking. Such a simple task to prove he is God, and yet he can't do it." The professor then dropped the chalk and watched it shatter dramatically on the classroom floor.

If you meet anyone who tries this silly trick, take the roof off. Apply the professor's logic in a test of *your own* existence. Tell the onlookers you will prove *you* don't exist.

Have someone take a piece of chalk and hold it above your outstretched palm. Explain that if you really exist, you would be able to accomplish the simple task of catching the chalk. When he drops the chalk, let it to fall the ground and shatter. Then announce, "I guess this proves I do not exist. If you believe in me, you're a fool."

Clearly, this chalk trick tells you nothing about God. The only thing it is capable of showing is that if God does exist, he is not a circus animal who can be teased into jumping through hoops to appease the whim of foolish people.

TROTTING OUT THE TODDLER

Virtually every argument in favor of abortion could equally justify killing newborns if pressed to its logical conclusion. If it's acceptable to take the life of an innocent human being on one side of the birth canal, why forbid it on the other? A 7-inch journey cannot miraculously transform a "nonhuman tissue mass" into a valuable human being.[6]

When someone justifies abortion by saying, "Women have the right to choose," use a version of Taking the Roof Off called "Trotting Out the Toddler." Ask if a woman should have the right to kill her one-year-old for the same reason.[7] Since both are human beings, the same moral rule should apply to each. The logic of choice, privacy, and personal bodily rights endangers newborns, not just the unborn.

At the University of New Mexico, a student said we should abort children to save them from future child abuse. Stand to Reason speaker Steve Wagner "trotted out the toddler" in response. "Should we also kill two-year-olds to save them from future child abuse?"

"I hadn't thought about that," the student said. And that's the point. People don't think about the logical implication of their ideas. It's our job to help them see their mistakes.

CLIMATE CONTROL

A chorus of voices charge that Christians, through their moralizing about homosexuality, are promoting a climate of hate. The phrase of choice is "less than." By claiming that homosexuality is wrong, Christians demote homosexuals to a "less than" status, making them the object of scorn, hatred, and physical abuse.

The flaw of this logic becomes obvious when you take the roof off. In Los Angeles, KABC talk show host Al Rantel — himself a homosexual — noted that this kind of thinking would make Alcoholics Anonymous responsible every time a drunk gets beat up in an alley. It simply does not follow that moral condemnation of homosexuality encourages gay-bashing.

Such a tactic is equally dangerous to those who use it. If moralizing causes hate, and hate leads to violence, are those who demonize Christians for condemning homosexuality also guilty of hate-mongering? Taking the Roof Off clearly demonstrates that this kind of attack is really about politics, not principles.

"FAITH" VS. FACTS

Some people think that facts and knowledge make faith impossible.

The reasoning goes like this. Hebrews 11:6 says that without faith, it is impossible to please God. Faith is believing things we cannot know. Faith and knowledge, then, are at opposite ends of the spectrum. The more facts we have, the less room there is for faith. God is most pleased, then, when we cling faithfully to our convictions in spite of the evidence against them.

If this is your view of faith, following this route will lead you into a spiritual ditch. First, apologetics — giving evidence in defense of the truth — would be misguided. This is scripturally absurd. Peter says we should always be ready to make an *apologia*, a defense, for our hope (1 Peter 3:15), and Jesus and the apostles gave evidence regularly.

Second, if knowledge and faith are inversely proportional (i.e., as knowledge decreases, faith increases), the more evidence we find *against* Christianity the better. Our knowledge would shrink to nothing, providing ample opportunity for an abundance of blind faith. Indeed, affirming something you knew to be false would be the greatest virtue, if you took this view. God would be most pleased with those who had every reason to know the resurrection never happened, for example, yet still believed.

The apostle Paul, however, called such a person pitiful:

> If Christ has not been raised ... your faith also is vain.... You are still in your sins. Then those also who have fallen asleep in Christ have perished. If we have hoped in Christ in this life only, we are of all men most to be pitied. (1 Corinthians 15:14, 17 – 19)

According to Paul, if we believe contrary to fact, we believe in vain. We are not heroes to be praised, but fools to be pitied.

What has gone wrong here? The problem is with the premise, "Faith is believing things we cannot know." This is not a biblical understanding of faith. Faith and knowledge are not opposites in Scripture. They are companions. The opposite of faith is not fact, but unbelief. The opposite of knowledge is ignorance. Neither is a virtue in Christianity.

EARTH DAY FOR EVOLUTIONISTS?

Has anyone else noticed a contradiction implicit in the annual Earth Day celebrations? The vast majority of devotees at such fetes are Darwinists who believe humans have an obligation to protect the environment. Starting with a naturalistic worldview, though, why should anyone care?

For millions of years, Mother Nature has spewed noxious fumes and poisonous gasses into Earth's atmosphere and littered the landscape with ash and lava. Indeed, the most "natural" condition in the universe is death. As far as we know, the Earth is completely unique. Death reigns everywhere else.

Species have passed into extinction at a steady rate from the beginning of time, the strong supplanting the weak. Why shouldn't they? Each is in a struggle for survival, a dance of destruction fueling the evolutionary process. May the best beast win. That's the logic of naturalism. Yet the sense of obligation to steward the Earth is strong. Why?

The moral motivation for Earth Day simply does not follow from Darwinism. It makes perfect sense, though, if God entrusted man with stewardship over the Earth. Taking the Roof Off—following an idea to its logical conclusion—shows that Earth Day makes sense for theists, but not Darwinists.

Here's a variation of the same idea. If there is no God and we evolved by chance, there is no fundamental difference between animals and humans. However, we permit a farmer to divide the weak from the strong in his pack of cows, yet we're appalled when Hitler does the same to Jews. Why is the first right, but the second wrong, given a Darwinian starting point?

"MODIFIED PRO-CHOICE"

The modified pro-choice position is a politician's favorite abortion doubletalk: "I'm personally against abortion, but I don't believe in forcing my view on others."

I once had a discussion with a man who offered this nonsense to me at a conference. I asked him the question I always pose when I encounter such a notion: "Why are *you* personally against abortion?"

He responded with the answer I always get. "I believe abortion kills a baby," he said, "but that's just my own personal view."

"Let me see if I understand you," I said. "You are convinced that abortion kills an innocent child, yet you think the law should allow women to do that to their own babies. Did I get that right?"

He objected to my wording, but when I asked him what part of his view I misunderstood, he was silent. I hadn't misunderstood it. That *was* his view.

> The logic of the modified pro-choice position reduces to, "I think it's wrong to kill my own children, but I don't think we should stop other people from killing theirs."

JUST YOUR INTERPRETATION

The "that's just your interpretation" parry when you make a biblical point is usually vulnerable to Taking the Roof Off. Use the first Columbo question ("What do you mean by that?") to find out if the person thinks all interpretations are equally valid and yours is just another in an infinite line of alternatives.

If you suspect that this is his view, Take the Roof Off. Treat his *own* words as infinitely malleable. Tell him, for example, that you are sorry to hear that he believes all Jews and homosexuals should be executed. When his jaw drops, tell him that's *your* interpretation of what he said. Does he have a problem with that?

Don't leave him hanging, though. Clarify your point: Some interpretations *are* better than others. If the person you are talking with thinks you have distorted the Scripture, then invite him to show you the error, not dismiss you with this weak response.

WHAT WE LEARNED IN THIS CHAPTER

Taking the Roof Off is a technique designed to show that some views prove too much. If taken seriously, they lead to counterintuitive or even absurd results. Another name for this tactic is *reductio ad absurdum*.

This tactic has three steps. First, we reduce the point of view to its basic argument, assertion, principle, or premise. Second, we give the idea a "test drive" to see if any absurd consequences result when we consistently apply the logic of the view. Third, we invite the person to consider the unusual implications of her view and the truth that follows from the reductio.

Taking the Roof Off works because humans are made in the image of God and must live in the world God created. Any person who denies this fact lives in tension between the way he *says* the world is and the way the world *actually* is. To protect himself from this contradiction, mankind has erected a self-deception — or a "roof" — to shield himself from the logical implications of his beliefs. With our tactic, we try to remove that roof to deprive him of his false sense of security, then show him the truth.

CHAPTER 11

STEAMROLLER

VERY few people quickly admit that their beliefs are wrong. Some put up a real fight even when your points are reasonable and your manner is gracious. Did you ever wonder why people do that? Why do people ignore good arguments?

I think there are four different reasons for resistance, and I would like to explain what those are. Then I will give you a step-by-step plan to deal with that overconfident, overbearing, and often overwhelming interrupter I call a "steamroller."

WHEN ARGUMENTS DON'T WORK

In chapter 2 I talked about the importance of arguments — not angry squabbles or silly quarrels, but points of view buttressed with reasons. Jesus used them. Paul used them. Peter used them. We should use them, too.

When arguments are done well, they honor God. But arguments have limits; they don't always work. When that happens, some people are tempted to think that arguments themselves are useless.

This is a mistake. If you're searching for that perfect line of logic capable of subduing any objection, you're wasting your time. There is no magic, no silver bullet, no clever turn of thought or phrase that's guaranteed to compel belief.

Yes, *rational reasons* can be a barrier to belief. The Christian message simply doesn't make sense to everyone, or it raises questions or counterexamples that make it difficult for some to even consider Christianity until those issues are addressed.

But rational appeals often fail to persuade for other reasons. At least three additional issues may compel the person you're talking with to ignore your point. They have nothing to do with clear thinking, even when objections based on reason are the first to surface. If your thoughtful response fails to have an impact, is not acknowledged — or, worse, doesn't even seem to have been noticed — maybe one of these reasons is lurking in the shadows.

First, people have *emotional reasons* to resist. Many have had annoying experiences with Christians or abusive churches. Others realize that to embrace Christianity would be to admit that cherished loved ones now dead entered eternity without forgiveness and with one fate awaiting them: darkness, despair, and suffering forever. Emotionally, this is something the person simply cannot bear.

Others know they would face the rejection of family and friends or perhaps suffer financial loss, physical harm, or even death if they considered Christ. These powerful deterrents can make the most cogent argument seem soft and unappealing.

Second, some balk because of *prejudice*. Their minds are already made up. They have prejudged your view before ever really listening to your reasons. They are interested in defending their own entrenched position, not considering other options.

Cultural influences are very powerful here. Resistance based on prejudice is especially true both of religious beliefs and of nonreligious beliefs (like naturalism) held with religious intensity. Often Christians defend their own denominational peculiarities in a very biased way. They plow ahead with blinders on, spouting the party line with no thought to the merits of the other side.

Finally, some people are just plain pigheaded. Their real reason for resistance is no more elegant or sophisticated than simple *rebellion*. Jesus said that people love the darkness rather than the light because their deeds are evil (John 3:19). So they persist in their mutiny, waging their unwinnable battle against God to the bitter end.

As you can see, you and I have very limited control over how other people respond to us. That is largely in God's hands. We can remove some of the negatives or dispel some of the fog — and we ought to try to do both. But at the end of the day, a person's deep-seated rebellion against God is a problem only a supernatural solution can fix.

When someone forcefully disagrees with you, do not expect him to surrender quickly. Changing beliefs is not easy to do, especially when a lot is at stake. Usually, it is a slow process for someone to admit they are mistaken about something important.

Sometimes a person's impulse to resist is so strong he will get verbally abusive. You need a plan to help keep you in control of conversations with those people who have controlling personalities and bad manners. This tactic is a defensive maneuver I call "Steamroller."

STEAMROLLER

Once in a while you will encounter people who try to overpower you. They don't overwhelm you with facts or arguments. Rather, they roll over you with the force of their personalities. Their challenges come quickly, one after another, keeping you from collecting your wits and giving a thoughtful answer.[1] If this description sounds familiar, then you have been steamrolled. Men are frequently guilty of steamrolling, especially when talking with women, but women can be offenders, too.

Steamrollers have a defining characteristic. They constantly interrupt. As soon as you begin to answer, they hear something they don't like in your explanation, interrupt, then pile on another challenge. If you try to go down the new path, they interrupt again, firing questions, changing the subject, yet never really listening to anything you say. You find yourself constantly off balance and on the defensive.

Though there are benevolent steamrollers — overly excitable, but not hostile — most are insincere. Steamrollers are not usually interested in answers. They are interested in winning through intimidation. It is easier for them to ask the hard questions than to listen to an answer that is more than a shallow, 10-second sound byte.

Because steamrollers are so aggressive, you must manage them aggressively, though you do not need to be rude. For some, it will take a little courage and intestinal fortitude to face up to such a powerhouse at first. However, once you learn the following three steps to stop a steamroller, you will discover that getting back into the driver's seat is easier than you thought.

Step One: Stop Him

The first step in dealing with a steamroller is a mild one. Even though you may feel pushed to your limits by the annoyance, don't fire back in kind, guaranteeing a head-on collision. Don't buckle at the knees, either. "Once your opponent has intimidated you and knows it, you've lost," says William Dembski, a veteran of many encounters with hostile challengers of intelligent design.[2]

Instead, your first move should be a genial request for courtesy. Stop the intrusion by momentarily putting the discussion on "pause." Then, briefly get permission to continue your point without being interrupted. Use a little body language if you need to, raising your hand a bit for emphasis.

It takes longer to describe it than to do it. Simply hold up your hand and gently say, "I'm not quite finished," and then continue. Often this is all you need to do to restore order to the conversation.

If the steamroller is especially aggressive, be calm and wait for an opening. Do not try to talk over him if he isn't cooperating at first. When you get a pause, don't be afraid to ask for adequate time. Quickly negotiate an informal agreement. You ask him to give *you* something — patience and courtesy — so that you can give *him* something in return — an answer. Here are some variations:

- "Is it okay with you if I take a few moments to answer your question before you ask another? I'll give you a chance to respond when I get done. Will that work?"
- "That's not a simple issue. I need a moment to explain myself. Is that okay?"
- "Let me respond to your first challenge. When I'm done, you can jump in again with another. Is that all right?"
- "That's a good question, and it deserves a decent answer, but that will take a few minutes. Are you okay with that?"

Notice the negotiation here. You make a petition, and he grants it. With more aggressive steamrollers, it is especially important for them to verbally consent to your request. (Of course, if a person answers "no" to any of these questions, you might ask him why he brought the challenge up in the first place.)

Be careful not to let annoyance or hostility creep into your voice. That would be a mistake, especially with this kind of person.

> Don't let a steamroller get under your skin. Being defensive and belligerent always looks weak. Instead, stay focused on the issues, not on the attitude. Talk calmly and try to look confident.

Be sure to respond adequately to one question before you are forced to tackle another, but don't take unfair advantage of the time you buy with this little negotiation. Make your point, then ask, "Does that make sense to you?" This invites him back into the conversation. Give him the courtesy of offering you a reply without interruption. You do not want to be a steamroller yourself.

Step Two: Shame Him

If the steamroller breaks trust with your agreement, or if you can't succeed in stopping him in the first place to negotiate an orderly conversation, proceed to phase two of the Steamroller tactic. This step is more aggressive. It also takes a bit more courage because you will now be directly confronting the rudeness of an impolite person. You might consider using his name at this point. It will soften the exchange.

> What's in a name? Plenty. A person's name is sweet to him. Keep this in mind when conversations begin to take a hostile turn. At the first sign of tension, pause and ask their name. Then use it in a friendly manner as you continue. It really helps take the edge off.

You tried to stop the steamroller. That didn't work. Now you want to shame him for his bad manners, but you want to do it with integrity. Start by taking the same basic approach you did in step one. This time, though, make an explicit request for courtesy.

First, ignore any new challenges he has introduced. Do not follow his rabbit trails. Second, address the steamroller problem directly. If you are not able to get the floor right away, let him talk. When he finally pauses, look him in the eye and calmly say something like this:

- "Can I ask you a favor? I'd love to respond to your concern, but you keep breaking in. Could I have a few moments without being cut off to develop my point? Then you can tell me what you think. Is that okay with you?" Wait for a response.
- "Can I ask you a quick question? Do you really want a response from me? At first I thought you did, but when you continue to interrupt I get the impression all you want is an audience. If so, just let me know and I'll listen. But if you want an answer, you'll have to give me time to respond. Tell me what you want. I need to know before I can continue." Wait for an answer.
- "Here's what I have in mind. You make your point, and I'll be polite and listen. When you're done, it will be your turn to be polite to me and not interrupt while I respond. Then, I'll let you

have your say without breaking in. I need to know if that's okay with you. If not, this conversation is over. What would you like to do?" Wait for a response.

Notice that each example I have offered is progressively more direct. You have to judge which one is necessary for the circumstances you face. The last one is very aggressive. If you started this way, you would be out of line. With some people, though, a direct approach like this is the only thing that will save the conversation. Use it only after the other person has used up a lot of grace.

Remember, steamrollers are strong customers who sometimes need to be addressed with equal strength, yet coupled with civility. This can be harder if you have a gentle spirit, but unless you toughen up at this stage, you'll get nowhere.

Step two should work. The steamroller might even be ashamed and apologize. Accept the gesture graciously, then return to the original issue and deal with it. Say, "Let's go back to the beginning. Your challenge as I understand it is this ... (repeat the question). Now, here is how I'd like to respond."

This second step is very effective in taming even the most belligerent steamroller. Don't be snippy or smug. Stay focused, stay pleasant, stay gracious, but stay in control.

If this doesn't work, go immediately to Step Three.

Step Three: Leave Him

First you *stop* him, then, you *shame* him. If that doesn't work, you *leave* him. When all else fails, let it go. Walk away. If the steamroller won't let you answer, listen politely until he's finished, then drop it. Let him have the satisfaction of having the last word, then shake the dust off your feet and move on. Wisdom dictates not wasting time with this kind of fool.

This last step is dictated by a simple bit of insight: Not everyone deserves an answer. This may sound odd at first. Characteristically, an ambassador is always ready, alert for any chance to represent

Christ, not backing away from a challenge or an opportunity. Sometimes, though, the wisest course of action may be to bow out graciously.

Jesus warned, "Do not give what is holy to dogs, and do not throw your pearls before swine" (Matthew 7:6). He followed his own advice, too. Jesus was amazingly tight-lipped before Pilate; he "gave him no answer" (John 19:9). At times, he was also evasive with religious leaders intent on tricking him: "Neither will I tell you by what authority I do these things" (Matthew 21:27).

Knowing when to step back requires the ability to separate the hogs and the dogs from the lost sheep looking for a shepherd. But how do you know when someone has crossed the line? When do we have an obligation to speak, and when should we save our pearls for another time?

Part of the answer can be found in Jesus' next words in Matthew 7:6: "… lest they trample [the pearls] under their feet, and turn and tear you to pieces." Be generous with the truth except with someone who shows utter contempt for the precious gift being offered him. He will simply trample it in the mud and then viciously turn on you.

If you sense someone pawing the turf and readying for a charge, it may be time to leave. Don't waste your efforts on people like this. There is plenty of ripe fruit waiting to be harvested. Save your energy for more productive encounters.

Of course, there are times when you will find yourself in a Jeremiah situation, being faithful to speak the truth even though it falls on deaf ears. But those occasions are not the rule. Usually, wisdom dictates we ration our efforts.

There is an exception to this principle, however. I have learned from my radio show that sometimes my real audience is not the person I'm talking to, but the people who are listening in, eavesdropping on the conversation.

This happens more often than you may think, even if you are not a radio host. Sometimes a word spoken to a hardened heart bounces off and hits a soft one. You may not even know that anyone else was listening. Years later, you discover that the Holy Spirit had a different audience in mind for your efforts. This has happened to me many times. Lee Strobel calls this "ricochet evangelism."

> When I face an aggressive challenger, I often give him the last word. Not only is this gracious, it's also powerful, conveying a deep sense of confidence in one's own view. Instead of fighting for the final say-so, give it away. Make your concluding point clearly and succinctly, and then say, "I'll let you have the last word." But don't break this promise. Grant him his parting shot, and then let it rest.

Dealing with a steamroller is rarely a smooth and tidy enterprise. When you encounter abuse, don't take it personally. It's not about you. It's about Christ. When you falter, don't get discouraged with the process. I get caught flat-footed too sometimes. Take it as a chance to learn for the next time around.

The principle? Make the best of the opportunities you have, then trust the Holy Spirit to be the witnessing partner who makes the difference. You do your part, then let God do his.

WHAT WE LEARNED IN THIS CHAPTER

In this chapter, we discovered that there was more than one reason a person might reject our arguments. There is nothing magical about a sound line of logic. For some people, reason doesn't matter. Some other barrier stands in the way.

Sometimes people have emotional reasons for resisting. Bad experiences with Christians or with churches, or pressures from family or culture are enough to blind a person to our appeals. Others balk because of prejudice. They never really consider our message because their minds are already made up. Finally, for many people, simple rebellion is the best explanation for rejection. The fundamental problem with most people is they do not want to bend the knee to their Sovereign.

Next, we learned how to recognize and restrain a steamroller. Steamrollers overpower you with strong personalities and interrupt constantly. We suggested three steps to manage a steamroller and put us back in control of the conversation. Step one, stop the interruption graciously but firmly, then briefly negotiate an agreement. Step two, shame him by making a very direct request for courtesy. Step three, leave. Never match a steamroller's incivility with rudeness. Instead, let him have the last word, then calmly walk away.

CHAPTER 12

RHODES SCHOLAR

IF you read magazines like *Time*, *U.S. News and World Report*, or *Newsweek*, you might have noticed a trend. Just before Easter and Christmas, these publications often feature cover stories about the history behind these two central events on the Christian calendar. The articles have provocative titles like, "What *Really* Happened to the Body of Jesus," or "The Untold Truth about the First Christmas." Generally, the authors take a what-scholars-say-that-your-pastor-does-not-want-you-to-know approach. They cite academics who use a "scientific" approach to history to expose the false notions held by the foolish faithful.

INFORMED OR EDUCATED?

Cover stories like these sell lots of magazines. They also discourage lots of Christians. Some wonder why these academic "facts" have been kept from them. Others don't know what to believe. They don't want to abandon their faith, but they cannot in good conscience dismiss the consensus of academic opinion simply because they don't like what they hear.

In situations like these, a tactic I call "Rhodes Scholar" is invaluable. It provides a way of knowing if an appeal to an authority is legitimate or not. The tactic hinges on the difference between *informing* and *educating*. When an article tells you *what* a scholar believes, you have been informed. When an article tells you *why* he holds his view, you have been educated.

Here is why this distinction is so important. If you recall from chapter 4, an argument is like a house whose roof (*what* a person believes) is supported by walls (the reasons *why* he believes). You cannot know if the reasons are adequate to the conclusions — if the walls are strong enough to hold the roof — unless you know what those reasons are. If you know the reasons, you can assess them. Without them, you're stonewalled.

Popular articles always inform, but almost never educate. As a result, you have no way of evaluating a scholar's conclusion. You simply have to take his word for it. But scholars can be wrong, and often are. Their reasoning can be weak, their facts can be mistaken, and bias can distort their judgment.

ASSESSING THE ACADEMICS

How do you know if an authority has been compromised? Regardless of a scholar's credentials, *always ask for reasons*. Don't settle for opinions. This is the key to Rhodes Scholar.

This tactic protects you from being victimized by a common error called the "fallacy of expert witness." There is nothing wrong with appealing to authority, but it must be done in the right way. You must ask, "Why should I believe this person's opinion?" There are two ways to answer this query.

First, the scholar may be in a special position to know the *facts*. However, if an authority is in possession of special information that guides his counsel, then he should be able to point to that evidence to convince us he's on the mark.

Sometimes authorities give opinions that are outside of their area of expertise. When California passed its controversial embryonic stem cell research initiative, twenty Nobel laureates backed the measure. Only four were listed by name and discipline. I looked carefully at their comments.

One, a professor of biology and physiology, assured voters that the measure was ethical. Another, a specialist in cancer research, said the legislation would boost California's economy and have a salutary impact on health care costs. An Alzheimer's research director promised new jobs and increased revenues for state coffers.

As I scanned the comments and credentials, it occurred to me that a Nobel Prize in biology, chemistry, or medicine does not qualify a person to render sound counsel on ethics or economics. This appeal to scholars was completely misdirected.

> Having twenty Nobel Prize winners on one's side may awe voters, but that fact alone does not legitimize the cause. You and I need more information before we can trust their endorsements.

Even when scholars speak within their field, they still owe us an accounting based on sound reasons. In a court of law, the expert witness is always cross-examined. Credentials alone are not enough to certify his testimony; he must convince a jury that his reasons are adequate. "All appeals to authority ultimately rest on the evidence the authority has," Norm Geisler says. "The letters after his name don't mean a thing without the evidence to back up his position."[1]

There's a second way the Rhodes Scholar query, "Why should I believe this person's opinion?" can be answered. Sometimes a scholar is in a unique position to render a *judgment*. More than mere facts are in play here. Interpretation is needed.

In this circumstance, you face another pitfall. A scholar's judgment may be distorted by underlying *philosophical* considerations that are not always on the table. Note this critique of pluralist John Hick's selective use of scholarship:

> Hick seems intent on deciding questions of great spiritual significance by counting scholarly noses ... without reminding readers that many of these scholars presuppose a picture of the world that excludes the possibility of divine intervention in the world.[2]

The point Doug Geivett makes here is that sometimes one's destination is *predetermined* by where one starts. If a scholar begins an investigation convinced that miracles cannot happen, it will be very difficult for him to conclude that something supernatural has taken place even when there is overwhelming evidence for it.

This problem is especially evident in science, where subjects like Darwinism and cosmology have worldview implications. The temptation is great to simply "count scholarly noses" without taking into consideration the powerful philosophical paradigm that dictates what kind of conclusions are acceptable.

TWO FACES OF SCIENCE

Whenever you hear the complaint, "Creation is not science," a subtle philosophical sleight of hand is in play. It capitalizes on an ambiguity between two completely different definitions of science.

The first definition is the most well known. Science is a *methodology* — observation, experimentation, testing — that allows researchers to discover facts about the world. Any view that does not follow the right methodology is not science. Presumably, this is why evolution succeeds and intelligent design fails.

The second definition of science involves the *philosophy* of naturalistic materialism. All phenomena must be explained in terms of matter and energy governed by natural law. Any view that does not conform to this second definition is also not science.

There are two requirements, then, for an investigation of the natural world to qualify as scientific. First, one must use the right methods. Second, one must come up with the right *kind* of answers, those consistent with materialism. Usually, these two elements are not in conflict. Good methods produce answers completely consistent with matter in motion governed by natural law. But sometimes they are not compatible. Evolution is a case in point.

> At first blush, it seems as if Darwinism is about scientific facts. But when facts suggest intelligent design, the second definition of science is surreptitiously invoked to label design as "unscientific."

Take note here: *When there is a conflict between methodology and materialism, the philosophy always trumps the facts.* Modern science does not *conclude* from the evidence that design is not tenable. It *assumes* it prior to the evidence. Any scientific methodology (first definition of science) that points to creation is summarily disqualified by scientific philosophy (second definition of science) as "religion disguised as science."

Douglas Futuyma, author of one of the most widely used college evolutionary biology textbooks, says, "Where science *insists on material, mechanistic causes* that can be understood by physics and chemistry, the literal believer in Genesis invokes *unknowable supernatural forces.*"[3]

Those who believe in intelligent design, however, claim that these forces are knowable, at least in principle. Consider this analogy. When a dead body is discovered, an impartial investigation might indicate foul play and not an accident. If the body is bullet-ridden, chances are the death was not a result of natural causes. In the same way, scientific evidence could, in principle, indicate an agent in creation rather than chance. This is not faith vs. evidence, but evidence vs. evidence.

Clearly, the materialist paradigm is paramount, and everything must be done to save it. Harvard Genetics Professor Richard Lewontin is amazingly candid about this fact. In the *New York Review of Books* he makes this stunning admission:

> Our willingness to accept scientific claims that are against common sense is the key to an understanding of the real struggle between science and the supernatural. We take the side of science *in spite of* the patent absurdity of some of its constructs ... *in spite of* the tolerance of the scientific community for

unsubstantiated just-so stories, because we have a prior commitment, a commitment to materialism. It is not that the methods and institutions of science somehow compel us to accept a material explanation of the phenomenal world, but, on the contrary, that we are forced by our *a priori* adherence to material causes to create an apparatus of investigation and a set of concepts that produce material explanations, no matter how counterintuitive, no matter how mystifying to the uninitiated. Moreover, that materialism is absolute, for we cannot allow a Divine Foot in the door.[4]

Here Lewontin admits that the apparatus of science is not geared to produce the truth, whatever it may be, but rather to produce philosophically acceptable answers. He openly admits that the game has been rigged.

Most who hold this prejudice are not so candid. In fact, the majority—confident their convictions rest on scientific fact not materialist philosophy—are not even aware of any problem. They show their hand, however, with telltale responses like "Creation is not science," or "Intelligent design is religion disguised as science."

These comments should always trigger questions: "*What specifically* disqualifies creation as science?" or "*Why* dismiss the idea of design in spite of the evidence?" Invariably, your Rhodes Scholar probing will reveal the real reason behind the rejection: bias, not fact. Creation of any sort is not the right *kind* of answer.

THE "HISTORICAL" JESUS

Science is not the only field where the game has been rigged. In the beginning of this chapter, I mentioned that this approach has also been applied to the Gospels. Whenever someone uses the word "scientific" to describe the way they look at history, they are signaling that materialistic philosophy governs the process.

Scholars from this school try to distinguish the Jesus of history from the miracle-working Jesus of faith. They assume, of course, there is a difference between the two. Why make this distinction?

In academics, everyone has a starting point. The place many scholars begin is not always clear to the public, but it is critical to understanding and evaluating their conclusions. Magazine stories about Easter are quick to point out that scholars reject the resurrection. But *why* do they reject it? A closer examination reveals their starting point. In a materialistic view of the universe, resurrections do not happen. Therefore, any reports of revived corpses must be myths added to the records years later.

Robert Funk of the Jesus Seminar makes this clear: "The Gospels are now *assumed* to be narratives in which the memory of Jesus is *embellished* by mythic elements that express the church's faith in him, and by *plausible fictions* that enhance the telling of the gospel story for first-century listeners."[5]

The reasoning often goes something like this: The Gospels contain fabrications because they record events that are inconsistent with a "scientific" (i.e., materialistic) view of the world. Resurrection accounts, then, are myth. Furthermore, if Jesus predicts an event that comes to pass decades after his death (the fall of Jerusalem in AD 70, for example), this must have been added after the event occurred, since prophecy (a kind of miraculous knowledge) is impossible. The Gospels, then, were written late and could not be eye-witness accounts.

Notice the significance of the starting point. When an academic begins with naturalism, a series of "facts" fall into place before any genuine historical analysis begins: The resurrection is an invention; the miracles are myths; there is no prophecy in the Bible; the Gospels were written long after the events took place and not by eyewitnesses. Starting with one's conclusions, though, is cheating. Nothing has been proved, only assumed.

Using the Rhodes Scholar tactic — asking for the scholar's reasons, not just his credentials — helps us flush out both the facts and the philosophy that may be corrupting the interpretation of the facts. This allows us to assess the scholar's opinion for ourselves rather than simply having to take it on faith.

Remember, reasons are more important than votes. If the reasoning is bad — if the facts are bad or the judgments are tainted by philosophic bias — it doesn't matter if you are talking with scholars or students, the view is still compromised.

NOT ALL BIAS IS EQUAL

Can the charge of bias be leveled at Christians? Certainly, and sometimes the charge is justified. Whenever someone has already taken sides on an issue, it is possible that he has not been even-handed in his analysis.

It is not fair, though, to assume someone has *distorted the facts* simply because he has a stake in the matter. People who are not neutral can still be fair and impartial. Instead, you have to show that they have faltered by looking carefully at the evidence itself.

Not all forms of bias are equal. When a Christian deals with issues like science and history, it's fair to say he's biased because he brings certain assumptions to the process like everyone else. A Christian's bias, though, does not inform his conclusions the same way that biases inform the conclusions of scientists or historians restricted by a commitment to materialism.

The current bias of science arbitrarily eliminates certain answers before the game gets started. Many scientists and historians *must* come up with conclusions that leave the supernatural out of the picture because their philosophy demands it.

A theist is not so encumbered. She believes in the laws of nature, but also is open to the possibility of supernatural intervention. Both are consistent with her worldview. She can judge the evidence on its own merits, unhindered by a philosophy that automatically eliminates supernatural options before the evidence receives a hearing.

Ironically, the Christian's bias *broadens* her categories making her *more* open-minded, not less. She has a greater chance of discovering truth because she can follow the evidence wherever it leads. That's a critical distinction. Can bias make a person open-minded? Under the right set of circumstances, absolutely.[6]

Ultimately, the issue isn't bias, but distortion. It's unsound, for example, to say that because the gospel writers were Christians, their testimony cannot be trusted. Conversely, a nonbeliever's conclusions should not be dismissed because he is not among the "faithful." In both cases, we have to look at the reasons themselves. This is the heart of Rhodes Scholar.

WHAT WE LEARNED IN THIS CHAPTER

The Rhodes Scholar tactic gives us a tool to use when someone invokes scholarly opinion against our view. It protects us from a common error called the "fallacy of expert witness."

On the one hand, appealing to scholarly opinion is a legitimate way to make a point. Sometimes an expert is in a unique position to know the facts or render a judgment. But experts are not always right. Be on the lookout for appeals to scholarship that are misapplied.

Sometimes authorities weigh in outside of their area of expertise. Other times they get their facts wrong, or philosophical bias distorts their judgment. The key to Rhodes Scholar is getting past the *opinion* of a scholar and probing the *reasons* for his opinions. This is the difference between being informed and being educated.

Whether an alleged expert is offering facts or judgments, always ask for an accounting. How did he come to his conclusions? What are the facts, specifically? Are there any biases that seem to be distorting their assessment? With the reasons on the table, you are in a better position to judge if a scholar's conclusions are sound.

Don't be shaken by academic airs. *What* an expert believes is not as important as *why* he believes it. Fancy credentials are not enough. What matters most are not the opinions, but the reasons.

CHAPTER 13

JUST THE FACTS, MA'AM

THERE is an old TV police drama called *Dragnet* that you may have heard of, but probably have never seen unless you are over fifty or watch reruns — really *old* reruns. Two lines from Dragnet are still remembered to this day. The first is, "The names have been changed to protect the innocent." The second is, "Just the facts, ma'am," Detective Joe Friday's trademark request of whomever he questioned as a witness.

Just the Facts, Ma'am is an easy tactic to use. It requires no cleverness or deft maneuvering. Only two things are necessary. First is the awareness that many challenges to Christianity are based on bad information. These objections can be overcome by a simple appeal to the facts. The second requirement is that you need to know the facts. If you do, you can beat the objection. This is not an absolute requirement for this tactic, because sometimes you can spot a wrong answer even though you don't know the right one. But knowing the right answer is central to using Just the Facts, Ma'am, and often that information is just a few keystrokes away.

Let me give you an example of a popular challenge to Christianity that is not based on fact, though many think it is. The protest goes something like this: "More wars have been fought and more blood has been shed in the name of God than any other cause. Religion is the greatest source of evil in the world."

Now, one might point out that even if this were the case, it is not entirely clear what conclusions about religion are justified from that data. You couldn't properly conclude, for example, that God does not exist or that Jesus was not the Savior simply by citing acts of violence done in the name of God or Christ.

> Since oppression and mayhem are neither religious duties for Christians nor logical applications of the teachings of Christ, violence done in the name of Christ cannot be laid at his door. This conduct might tell you something about **people**. It tells you nothing about **God** or **the gospel**.

So there are logical problems with this complaint, but the bigger problem is that this charge is simply not true. Religion has *not* caused more wars and bloodshed than anything else in history.

Though it is easy to characterize religion as a blood-thirsty enterprise replete with witch hunts, crusades, and religious jihad, the historical facts show that the greatest evil has always resulted from *denial* of God, not *pursuit* of him. In the twentieth century alone, Dennis Prager notes, "more innocent people have been murdered, tortured, and enslaved by secular ideologies — Nazism and communism — than by all religions in history."[1]

Grab an older copy of the *Guinness Book of World Records* and turn to the category "Judicial," subheading "Crimes: Mass Killings." You'll find that carnage of unimaginable proportions resulted not from religion, but from institutionalized atheism: over 66 *million* wiped out under Lenin, Stalin, and Khrushchev; between 32 and 61 *million* Chinese killed under Communist regimes since 1949; one third of the eight million Khmers — 2.7 *million* people — were killed between 1975 and 1979 under the communist Khmer Rouge.[2]

> The greatest evil has not come from people zealous for God. It has resulted when people are convinced there is no God they must answer to.

I want you to notice something about the facts I cited above. They were as precise as I could make them without being cumbersome. I gave you a specific source with exact numbers and clear-cut dates. Precision is an important element of Just the Facts, Ma'am because of a foundational principle of persuasion: When citing facts in your defense, *precise numbers are always more persuasive than general figures.*

Though your memory may not always be up to the task (mine certainly isn't), always use the specific rather than the general when you can. When you communicate with factual precision, you convince your listeners that you know what you are talking about. Saying "Thousands died in the terrorist attacks of 9/11" is not as compelling as saying "2,973 human beings were buried beneath the rubble of the World Trade Center, the Pentagon, and a field in Pennsylvania on September 11, 2001." Each bit of precision — "2,973," "September 11, 2001," the specific locations of the attacks — adds force to your facts. It may take longer to say it, but with proper delivery, it is much more compelling.

This kind of exactness can be a powerful persuader. For example, I was once involved in a head-to-head encounter, of sorts, with Pulitzer Prize–winning historian Garry Wills before San Francisco's liberal Commonwealth Club, which was taped for national broadcast on NPR. In his opening salvo on the topic "Christianity in America," Professor Wills disputed the idea that the Founding Fathers of our republic were Christians. They were not Christians, he claimed, but deists.

The microphone was then passed to me. Fortunately, I had my facts. "The phrase 'Founding Fathers' is a proper noun," I explained. "It refers to a specific group: the delegates to the Constitutional Convention. There were other important players not in attendance, but these fifty-five made up the core." I then continued citing from memory, the best I could, the following facts that were a matter of public record: Among the delegates were twenty-eight Episcopalians, eight Presbyterians, seven Congregationalists, two Lutherans, two Dutch Reformed, two Methodists, two Roman Catholics, one unknown, and only three deists — Williamson, Wilson, and Franklin. This took place at a time when church membership usually entailed "sworn adherence to strict doctrinal creeds."[3]

This tally proves that 51 of 55 — a full 93 percent — of the members of the Constitutional Convention, the most influential group of men shaping the political underpinnings of our nation, were Christians, not deists.

> Virtually every person involved in the founding enterprise of the United States was a God-fearing Protestant whose theology in today's terms would be described as evangelical or "fundamentalist."

When I was finished, I set my microphone down and waited, bracing for the rebuttal from my learned opponent. But he said nothing. After a few moments of awkward silence, the moderator moved on to a new topic. Dr. Wills had his facts wrong. Mine were not only correct, but they were precise, adding tremendous persuasive power to my rebuttal.

FOLLOWING A PLAN

Challenges to Christianity that fail due to faulty facts may seem difficult to spot at first, especially if you are not well versed in the issue in question. But the task becomes much easier if you have a plan, a series of steps to guide your effort. For Just the Facts, Ma'am, I use the same two-step plan, whether I am having a conversation or doing a more detailed analysis of a book or article.

First ask, *"What is the claim?"* This may seem like an obvious initial step, but you'll be surprised how often we charge ahead without having a clear fix on a target. Take a moment to isolate the precise point being made. Write it down in unambiguous terms if you need to. Sometimes the claim is clear, but not always. Assertions are often implicit or hidden under a layer of rhetoric and linguistic maneuvering. Pay careful attention to get a clear fix on exactly what the person is asserting.

For example, a piece written by a student in a university newspaper claimed that pro-lifers had no right to oppose abortion unless they were willing to care for the children born to mothers in crisis pregnancies. Notice that the author was making two assertions here. The first was the obvious moral point, which was easily dispatched. In my written response to the paper, I pointed out that it simply does not follow that because a person objects to killing innocent children, he is obliged to care for those that survive. Imagine how bizarre it would sound to argue, "You have no right to stop me from beating my wife unless you're willing to marry her." Clearly, the offender is not off the hook simply because others won't step in to take his place. Implicit in the challenge, though, was a second assertion: the claim that pro-lifers were *not* doing anything for pregnant women who carried their babies to term. The student therefore felt justified criticizing the pro-life movement.

This brings us to the second step of our plan. Once the assertion is clear, ask, *"Is the claim factually accurate?"* Sometimes answering this question takes a little investigation. A short trip to the Internet revealed there were roughly four thousand national and international pro-life service providers dedicated to the well-being of mothers in crisis pregnancies who choose life for their children. They provide medical aid, housing, baby clothing, cribs, food, adoption services — even post-abortion counseling services — all at no cost. Amazingly, there were more crisis pregnancy centers in the country than abortion clinics. A quick check of the local phone directory showed there were ten right in the same city as the university. I pointed out each of these facts in my response to show there was no factual basis for the student's objection.

CRACKING THE CODE

I followed my two-step plan when evaluating the historical claims of the blockbuster novel, *The Da Vinci Code*, whose broadside on Christianity and the Bible created a public sensation, along with tremendous turmoil for Christians. First, I isolated the claims. The author, Dan Brown, made it simple in most cases by stating his contentions clearly.[4] Here are some of them:

- In the first three centuries, the warring between Christians and pagans threatened to rend Rome in two.
- The doctrine that Jesus was the Son of God was fabricated for political reasons at the Council of Nicaea in AD 325 and affirmed by a close vote.
- Constantine arranged for all gospels depicting Jesus as a mere mortal to be gathered up and destroyed.
- The Dead Sea Scrolls found in a cave near Qumran in the 1950s confirm that the modern Bible is a fabrication.
- Thousands of Christ's followers wrote accounts of Jesus' life. These evolved through countless translations, additions, and revisions. History has never had a definitive version.[5]

Because I now had specific items to assess, my job was much easier. The first challenge was simple. Even a cursory analysis of this period of history reveals there were no wars between pagans and Christians, and for a very good reason. Jesus' followers had neither armies nor the will to resist. Instead, they considered it a privilege to be martyred for Christ. They wouldn't even fight tormentors like Diocletian, who executed Christians by the thousands just twenty years before Constantine.

The Council of Nicaea was not an obscure event in history. We have extensive records of the proceedings written by those who were actually there: Eusebius of Caesarea and Athanasius, deacon of Alexandria. Two things stand out in those accounts that pertain to Brown's claims. First, *no one* at Nicaea considered Jesus to be a "mere mortal," not even Arius, whose errant views made the council necessary. Second, Christ's deity was the *reason* for the council, not merely the *result* of it.

After a pitched debate, the orthodox party prevailed. The vote wasn't close at all; it was a landslide. Of 318 bishops, only the

Egyptians Theonas and Secundus refused to concur.[6] The council affirmed what had been taught since the beginning. Jesus was not a mere man; he was God the Son.

Regarding the famous Dead Sea Scrolls, Brown might be forgiven for not getting the date right (the first scrolls were discovered in the 1940s, not the 1950s). There is no excuse, however, for another misstep: *The Dead Sea Scrolls say nothing of Jesus.* There were no Gospels in Qumran. Not one shred or shard mentions his name. This is a complete fabrication.

As for the rest of the claims, I want to let you in on a little secret. Answering the second question — Is the claim factually accurate? — does not always require investigation. I mentioned earlier that sometimes it is possible to spot a wrong answer even when you do not know the right one.

Before beginning any research, first ask, *"Does anything about the assertion seem suspicious or unlikely on its face?"* For example, early in *The Da Vinci Code*, Brown claims that over a period of three hundred years the Catholic Church burned five million witches at the stake in Europe around the fifteenth century.[7] I was immediately suspicious of this "fact," so I quickly took out my calculator and did the math. Rome would have to burn forty-five women a day, every single day, non-stop for three hundred years. That's a lot of firewood.

Furthermore, a quick Internet search revealed that the population for Europe at the time was about 50 million. If half were female (25 million) and half of those were adults (12.5 million), then something like *40 percent of the entire adult female population perished* at the hand of the Vatican. That's more carnage than the Black Plague of 1347, which killed only one-third. Let's just say this seems highly unlikely.

Many of Dan Brown's other claims can be quickly dispatched using the same technique:

- If the deity of Christ was an idea invented by Constantine and completely foreign to Christ's followers who viewed him as a mere mortal, what explains the "relatively close vote" at Nicaea?

- If the early records of Jesus' life are so corrupted and compromised with "countless translations, additions, and revisions," and if "history has never had a definitive version of the book," from where does Brown derive his reliable, authentic, unimpeachable biographical information about Jesus?
- How does Brown know that thousands of Jesus' followers wrote accounts of his life if the great bulk of these records were destroyed? This is the classic problem for conspiracy theorists. If all evidence was eradicated, how do they know it was there in the first place?
- How is it physically possible for Constantine to gather up all of the handwritten copies from every nook and cranny of the Roman empire by the fourth century and destroy the vast majority of them?

Each of these difficulties becomes obvious when you take a moment to ask if anything about the claim seems suspicious or implausible on its face. Granted, sometimes unlikely things turn out to be true, but when that's the case, the evidence has to be very precise and convincing. Usually, this question can save you some sleuthing.

ABORTION AND HOMICIDE

Here's another challenge that can be overcome by a simple appeal to facts. Some denounce the use of the word "murder" to describe abortion. Yet this language is completely consistent with the laws in nearly two-thirds of the states in the United States, at least in one regard. In the California statutes, for example, under the category "Crimes against the Person," §187, murder is defined this way: "Murder is the unlawful killing of a human being, *or a fetus*, with malice aforethought" (emphasis mine). After the definition, we find among the exceptions: "This section shall not apply to any person who commits an act which results in the death of a fetus if … the act was solicited, aided, abetted, or consented to by the mother of the fetus."

This exception in the California statute is troubling. The moral principle underlying all homicide statues is that human beings have innate worth. Value is not derived from something outside of the person; it is intrinsic. That's why destroying a human being is the most serious of crimes.

> Fetal homicide statutes like California's are odd because the only difference between legal abortion and punishable homicide is the consent of the mother.

If the *intrinsic* value of unborn human beings qualifies them for protection under homicide statutes, why is something *extrinsic*, like the mother's choice, relevant? How does the mere consent of the mother change the innate value of the little human being inside her?

However one answers this question, two facts remain. One, abortion is legal in states like California. Two, apart from the stipulated exceptions, killing the unborn is homicide. Those who do so are prosecuted for murder.

On the use of the word "murder," then, pro-lifers are not extreme. They agree with the statutes of the majority of states in this country: Unborn children are valuable human beings due the same protection as the rest of us. The problem is not with pro-life "extremists," but with inconsistent laws.

JUST THE CONTEXT, MA'AM

Resolving a challenge by appealing to the facts works with scriptural issues, too. Here's an example. I have been asked why God prohibits killing in the Ten Commandments, but then commands killing when the Jews take Canaan. That sounds like a contradiction.

It would be if not for a simple fact. The Fifth Commandment does not read "You shall not kill," but rather, "You shall not murder" (Exodus 20:13). There are different words for each in Hebrew just as in English, for a good reason. There is a moral distinction between *justified* killing (killing in self-defense, for example) and *unjustified* killing (murder). God prohibits the second, not the first. The facts show there is no contradiction.

When I debated the New Age author Deepak Chopra on national TV, he made an unusual statement about the text of the New Testament. He claimed that the King James Version was the eighteenth or nineteenth iteration of the Bible since the year 313.[8] This comment reflected, I think, the idea many people have that the New Testament has gone through a series of translations and retranslations — "iterations" — before finally settling into the English versions we have today.

A simple appeal to the facts was all I needed to dispatch Dr. Chopra's challenge. All current English translations of the Bible start with manuscripts written in the original language — Greek, in the case of the New Testament — which are then translated directly into English. Instead of multiple "iterations," there is only one step in language from the original Greek to our English versions.

Here's another example of applying Just the Facts, Ma'am to a passage that is almost universally misunderstood: "Do not judge lest you be judged" (Matthew 7:1). This is a verse everybody knows and quotes when convenient, even if they do not usually abide by the Bible. Jesus qualified this command, though, in a way that most do not:

> And why do you look at the speck that is in your brother's eye, but do not notice the log that is in your own eye? ... You hypocrite, first take the log out of your own eye, and then you will see clearly to take the speck out of your brother's eye. (Matthew 7:3, 5)

A closer look at the facts of the context shows that Jesus did not condemn all judgments, only hypocritical ones — arrogant condemnations characterized by disdain and condescension. Not all judgments are of this sort, so not all judgments are condemned. In fact, even in this passage Jesus actually encourages a different sort of judgment once the hypocrisy has been dealt with (*"first take the log out of your own eye, then you will see clearly to take the speck out of your brother's eye"*).

There are two other kinds of judging that *are* commanded in Scripture. *Judgments that are judicial* in nature are good when done by the proper authorities. Judges judge. They pass sentence. That's their job. Church discipline is of this sort.[9] Paul specifically warns us not to judge nonbelievers, but believers. God will judge the world in his time (1 Corinthians 5:12–13). Jesus himself did not come initially for this kind of judgment — he offered mercy, not sentencing — but he will certainly return with this kind. Appointed by the Father as final judge, he will spare no one.[10]

Judgments that are assessments — appraisals of right or wrong, wise or foolish, accurate or inaccurate, rational or irrational — are also commanded. Jesus' instructions "Do not give what is holy to dogs" (Matthew 7:6) require this kind of evaluation (What is "holy"? Who are the "dogs"?). Peter reminds us to "be of sound judgment" since "the end of all things is at hand" (1 Peter 4:7).

Some assessments are moral. Paul commands this kind of judgment in some circumstances: "Do not participate in the unfruitful deeds of darkness, but instead even expose them" (Ephesians 5:11). Jesus said this is to be done, not "according to appearance," but by "righteous" standards (John 7:24). He chastised the Jews for their failures here: "And why do you not even on your own initiative judge what is right?" (Luke 12:57).

A judicial action, a factual assessment, a hypocritical arrogance — all are judgments. Only the third is disqualified by Jesus. The first two are actually virtues in their proper settings and therefore commanded by Scripture. Those are the scriptural facts.

WHAT WE LEARNED IN THIS CHAPTER

As you can see, many who challenge Christianity base their case on ignorance or error. They simply have their facts wrong. Just the Facts, Ma'am is a maneuver you can use to help determine when this happens. In this chapter, we learned how to apply the two-step approach of this tactic.

Whenever a challenge to your view is based on an alleged factual claim (i.e., "More blood has been shed in the name of religion than anything else," or "America's Founding Fathers were deists"), first ask, "What is the precise claim?" These two examples are clear, but sometimes assertions are hidden. Separate the precise point or points from the rest of the rhetoric. Ask questions to make sure you know exactly what the person is alleging. (You might have noticed that this step is the same as the first step of Columbo.)

Next, ask if the facts are accurate. There are two ways to find mistakes. The Internet is the most convenient place to do quick research. Once you have isolated specific claims, verification is often a few keystrokes away. You may also have reference books or learned friends you can turn to.

You might save some time, though, by asking a different question before you start your sleuthing: Does anything about the claim seem unlikely or implausible on its face? If a dentist claims he has filled half a million cavities in his twenty-year career, you know he's confused. Just do the math.

Now, armed with the facts, you will be ready to address your friend's concerns. Keep in mind that when citing facts in your defense, precise numbers are always more persuasive than general figures.

In short, listen and read critically, reflect on the claims, check the background information, and find the truth. Like Detective Joe Friday, always say, "Just the facts, ma'am."

CHAPTER 14

MORE SWEAT, LESS BLOOD

AT the beginning of this book I made a promise. I said I would guide you, step by step, through a game plan that would help you maneuver comfortably and graciously in conversations about your Christian convictions.

I wanted to give you the tools to help make your engagements with others look more like diplomacy than like D-Day. I suggested an approach I called the Ambassador Model. It traded on friendly curiosity rather than confrontation. Then I introduced you to a handful of effective tactics to help you navigate in conversations.

I have done my best to keep my promise. Reading this book, though, does not guarantee that anything will be different in your conversations. That will be up to you. I want to talk now about your next steps.

When I was younger, I was an army reservist during the Vietnam era. If I were joining the military now, though, I think I would choose the marines. Two things about the marines impress me.

The first is the motto of the U.S. Marine Corps: *Semper Fi*. This is short for *semper fidelis*, a Latin phrase that means "Always faithful." The second is a training maxim I learned from a former marine who picked it up during the rigors of officer candidate school. This adage is in the back of my mind every time I prepare for a public encounter with an opponent who is dedicated to defeating my convictions: *"The more you sweat in training, the less you bleed in battle."*

I want to end this book with some suggestions that will help you sweat more and bleed less, and thus stay "always faithful" to the task ahead of you.

First, I would like to offer eight insights I gained from a conversation I overheard while flying home from vacation one summer. Next, I want to explain the best way I know to build a small fellowship of like-minded ambassadors for Christ who value the life of the mind. Finally, I want to share with you some lessons about the importance of hostile opposition and what I learned about courage under fire from a pair of timid door-to-door cult evangelists.

EIGHT QUICK TIPS

On a flight back from the Midwest, I listened while a Christian brother in the row directly behind me vigorously shared his faith with passengers on either side. I was glad for his effort (my wife and I were both praying for him), and he made some fine points. But some of his tactics were questionable. Here are some things I learned from that experience that might make your own efforts more effective.

First, be ready. The Christian brother behind me was clearly on the alert for chances to represent Christ. Seated between two other passengers, he had a captive audience on either side for almost four hours, and he was determined to make the most of the opportunity.

Though you do not need to squeeze each encounter dry (as he seemed to be doing), you should be willing at least to test the waters to see if there is any interest. Good ambassadors are vigilant, always watchful for what might turn out to be a divine appointment.

Second, keep it simple. On the way to sharing about the cross, our Christian passenger ranged from young-earth creationism to Armageddon. That is a lot to have to chew on to get to Jesus. The basic gospel is challenging enough. Generally, you will have to deal with a few obstacles that come up. But if the listener is interested, why complicate things with controversial issues unrelated to salvation? Remember, you want to put a stone in his shoe, not a boulder. If other issues don't come up, don't bring them up.

Third, avoid religious language and spiritual pretense. Our dear brother was obviously a Christian. His dialog was littered with spiritual lingo and religious posturing. Everything about his manner screamed "fundamentalist." Even when this is genuine, it sounds weird to outsiders. Words and phrases like "saved," "blessed," "the Word of God," "receive Christ," or "believing in Jesus as Savior and Lord," may have meaning to you, but they are tired religious clichés to everyone else.

Experiment with fresh, new ways to characterize the ancient message of truth. Consider using the word "trust" instead of "faith," or "follower of Jesus" instead of "Christian." I try to avoid quoting "the Bible." Instead, I quote the words of "Jesus of Nazareth" (the Gospels), or of "those Jesus trained to take his message after him" (the rest of the New Testament).

Avoid spiritual schmaltz like the plague. Even though a person is attracted to Christ, he may still be reluctant to join an enterprise that makes him look odd. Don't let your style get in the way of your message.

Next, focus on the truth of Christianity, not merely its personal benefits. I appreciated our evangelist's focus on truth rather than on experience. When one of his fellow passengers said he liked reincarnation, the Christian noted that "liking" reincarnation could not make it true. The facts matter. By focusing on the truth claims of Jesus instead of making a more subjective appeal, he gave his message a solid foundation.

Give reasons. This brother understood that making assertions without giving evidence would be an empty effort. He was ready to give the support needed to show that his claims were not trivial. Jesus, Paul, Peter, John, and all the prophets did the same. Even in a postmodern age, people still care about reasons.

Stay calm. Don't get mad. Don't show frustration. Don't look annoyed. Keep your cool. Our friend stayed composed the entire time. The more collected he was, the more confident he appeared. The more confident he seemed, the more persuasive he sounded.

If they want to go, let them leave. When you sense the one you are talking to is looking for an exit, back off a bit. Signs of waning interest — wandering eyes, a caged look, darting glances toward the doorway — are clues she's probably not listening anymore. Don't force the conversation. Instead, let the exchange end naturally. Remember, you don't need to close the sale in every encounter. God is in charge. He will bring the next ambassador along to pick up where you left off. When the conversation becomes a monologue (yours), it's time to let it go.

But don't let them leave empty-handed. If possible, give the person a tangible way to follow up on what you challenged him to consider. Our friend had an arsenal of tracts, booklets, and Christian paperbacks to leave behind to keep the thinking process going. You might offer your business card, a Christian Web site (e.g., www.str.org), or something to read. A copy of the Gospel of John is a good choice. It's small, inexpensive, and focuses on Christ. Offer it as a gift, suggesting, "It might be best for me to let Jesus speak for himself."

These eight ideas remove obstacles that get in your way as an ambassador. They will make it easier for others to focus on your message without being distracted by your methods. The irony is that when our method is skillful, it fades into the background. But when our method is clumsy or offensive, then *it* becomes the focus instead of the truth we want to communicate.

DRY TINDER

Another key to making you a better ambassador is the company you keep. You may have found that this book has opened up a whole new spiritual landscape that you are anxious to explore.

This can be exhilarating, but it can also be frustrating if your Christian friends have not experienced the same epiphany. There is a solution, though.

A while back, I spent most of one day with seven seemingly ordinary women who captured my attention, respect, and admiration. They were not philosophers, theologians, authors, or captains of industry. They were mostly mothers and housewives juggling carpools, laundry, and tired husbands.

Every couple of weeks they gathered together with their Bibles and study materials in a small group simply known as "Women of Berea." Their main purpose was not prayer or fellowship, though both of those things happened. Rather, their goal was study and discussion, engaging their minds in careful thinking on things that mattered.

When people ask me how to get their church interested in loving God with their minds as Christians, I have a simple bit of advice that these women understood: *You can't start a fire with wet wood. You must begin with dry tinder.*

In nearly every church there are brothers and sisters who share your hunger, but have yet to share your discovery. They are dissatisfied, yearning for something more substantial, but do not know where to turn. These people are your dry tinder.

Do not make it your goal to change your church just yet. First, find these people. Gather up the dry tinder, plant your own spark, and kindle a flame. Aim to start a modest fire with a cluster of believers of kindred spirit who value using their minds in their pursuit of God. Once the fire gets ignited, don't be surprised if some of the wet wood dries out and begins to blaze.

Commit to meet together on a regular basis: weekly, biweekly, monthly — whatever fits your schedules. Individual commitments to your group may be short-term for a particular study project or part of a long-term relationship similar to C. S. Lewis's friendships with J. R. R. Tolkien and others in a group they called the "Inklings." It's up to you.

"Culture is most profoundly changed," Chuck Colson says, "not by the efforts of huge institutions, but by individual people."[1]

Edmund Burke calls them "little platoons," small groups of ordinary folks making a difference where their feet hit the sidewalk.

Meet together for a limited but definite period of time to study a particular topic. You might listen to tapes as a group or discuss a book. You might role-play differences of opinion, using the tactics you have learned from this book. Or you might work together to construct an intelligent, reasoned response to the specific points you heard on a talk show or saw in a letter to the editor. Encourage each other to step out of your comfort zones and apply what you're learning.

Your group could become a catalyst influencing others in your church, a vital resource that your Christian friends can turn to when they have questions. The Women of Berea soon began to have an impact beyond their own ranks, drying out the wet wood around them because they were good ambassadors for the Christian faith. The key to effectiveness outside your group is to stay visible, be committed to excellence, and keep a good attitude. This is not a time for pride, but a time for usefulness.

Remember, look for the dry tinder — like-minded people of kindred spirit. There are more of them than you may think. You just have to find them. You could be the match that kindles the tinder that starts a holy bonfire in your own church. You just need to be willing to take the initiative to lead others in the pursuit of a more intelligent faith.

HOSTILE WITNESSES

Part of that pursuit involves a certain kind of vulnerability. None of us wants our views proven wrong, especially our most cherished ideas, regardless of which side of the fence we are on. But if we want to cultivate a well-informed faith, we need to be aware of our own powerful instincts for ideological self-preservation.

This instinct is so strong, in fact, that sometimes we are tempted to intellectually circle the wagons and guard against the slightest challenge to our beliefs. This strategy provides a false sense of security, however. The opposite approach actually offers much more safety. Instead of digging in behind fortifications to protect against attackers, we should encourage critique by hostile witnesses.

In academic circles, this is called "peer review." Philosophers, scientists, and theologians present their ideas in professional forums and solicit critique. They test the merit of their thoughts by offering them to people who are inclined to disagree.

A few years ago, I attended a three-day conference titled "Design and Its Critics." The best minds in the intelligent design movement were assembled to make their case. But they were not alone. They had invited the top Darwinian thinkers in the country to listen to their ideas and take their best shots. It was one of the most invigorating and intellectually honest encounters I have ever witnessed.

> Peer review is based on a sound notion. If our ideas are easily destroyed by those acquainted with the facts, they ought to be discarded. But if our ideas are good, they will not be upended so easily. In the process, we will learn what the other side knows. We may even be surprised at how weak their resistance really is.

The lesson of hostile witnesses was driven home to me quite unexpectedly one day. While sitting in my own library prepping for my Sunday afternoon radio show, I heard a knock on my front door. When I answered, two middle-aged women smiled at me pleasantly, bundles of apocalyptic literature in hand. They asked if I wanted to see their material.

I mentioned that there were two at the door, but only the one in front — the one who had knocked — spoke. The second stood quietly in the back, watching. Jehovah's Witnesses go out in pairs, usually one experienced Witness and one new disciple. The neophyte makes the initial contact, while the mentor waits protectively in the background, ready for a flanking maneuver if the young cadet gets into trouble.

I knew the encounter would be brief. First, I had little time to make an impact because I had to leave for the radio studio. Second, door-to-door missionaries like these usually have little time for anyone who is biblically literate. Once I showed my hand, I knew they would disappear quickly and look for an easier mark. Still, I did not want to send my visitors away empty-handed.

"I am a Christian," I began. I directed my comments to the younger convert, the one less influenced by the Watchtower organization and probably more open to another viewpoint.

"It's clear we have some differences, including the vital issue of the identity of Jesus. I believe what John teaches in John 1:3, that Jesus is the uncreated Creator. This would make him God."[2]

Mention of the deity of Christ was all that was needed to bring the rear guard into action. The woman in the shadows spoke up for the first time. I honestly wasn't prepared for her response. "You're entitled to your opinion, and we're entitled to ours," was all she said. No question, no challenge, no theological rebuttal. This was a dismissal, not a response. She turned on her heel and started for the next house, trainee in tow, in search of more vulnerable game.

I cast about for something to say that might slow their retreat. "You're also entitled to be wrong in your opinion," I blurted out, but the retort had no effect. I admit it probably was a poor response, but it was all I could think of at the moment. "Clearly we both can't be right," I added, trying to mend the breach, "even though we're both entitled to our opinions."

I was hoping for some kind of reaction, some kind of engagement, but my challenge went unanswered. As they marched down the walkway, I fired my final salvo, vainly hoping for a response: "Obviously, you're not interested in hearing any other point of view than your own." Then they were gone.

GUN SHY

In the moments that followed, a host of questions flooded my mind. Did I use the right tactic? Would a different approach have been more effective? Did anything I say make a good impression? Did I plant even a seed of doubt in their minds? I will probably never know the answer to those questions, but the meeting was still educational. Notice a couple of things about this short exchange.

What did these two missionaries do when they encountered someone who was biblically literate? What was their first response when I mentioned my background and then gave a thumbnail sketch of an argument striking at the heart of their most cherished doctrine? They backed off. They bailed out. They ran away. What's wrong with this picture?

If you were convinced that the medicine you held in your hand would save the life of a dying patient, would you turn away, letting him perish because he did not like the taste of the treatment? In the same way, isn't it strange that a door-to-door evangelist out to save the world would take flight at the first sign of any opposition? These Jehovah's Witnesses missionaries were in a battle for human souls, yet they fled at the first sound of gunfire.

This encounter taught me three things about these missionaries that were also lessons for me. First, they were not confident in their message. Why should I take a single moment to consider their alleged message from God if the messenger herself would not lift a finger to defend it? Why should I respect the cause of a soldier who retreats at the first sign of resistance?

Second, these missionaries could not have been interested in my salvation. If they were genuinely concerned about rescuing my lost soul, their first impulse would be to find out what I thought and why, then attempt to correct my errant theology. Isn't that why they go door-to-door, to witness to the lost, to give them the truth about God as they understand it? Yet they did not even listen to my point of view, much less try to correct my error. That tells me they didn't care much about my eternal destiny.

Third, I learned that they did not take the issue of truth seriously. Religious evangelism is a persuasive enterprise. The evangelist thinks her view is true and opposing views are false. She also thinks the difference matters, which is why she is trying to change other people's minds. Follow the truth, you win; follow a lie, you lose — big time.

A commitment to truth — as opposed to a commitment to an organization — means an openness to refining one's own views. It means increasing the accuracy of one's understanding and being open to correction in thinking. A challenger might turn out to be a blessing in disguise, an ally instead of an enemy. An evangelist who is convinced of her view, then, should be willing to engage the best arguments *against* it.

One of two things would then happen. She may discover that some objections to her view are good ones. The rebuttal helps her make adjustments and corrections in her thinking, refining her knowledge of the truth. Or it may turn out she is on solid ground after all. Developing answers to the toughest arguments against her position strengthens both her witness and her confidence in her convictions.

COURAGE UNDER FIRE

Here is the lesson: Don't retreat in the face of opposition. Too much is at stake. Be the kind of soldier who instills respect in others because of your courage under fire. Make your case in the presence of hostile witnesses. Throw your gauntlet into the arena and see what the other side has to say. It's one of the most effective ways to establish your case and to help you cultivate a bullet-proof faith over time.

Do not lose heart if your audience seems to get the best of you sometimes. There is an easy explanation for why we sometimes feel ill-treated or ignored, a simple reason why the scoreboard often reads, "Lions – 10, Christians – 0." Jesus warned us in advance: "A disciple is not above his teacher, nor a slave above his master.…

If they have called the head of the house Beelzebul, how much more the members of his household!" (Matthew 10:24–25).

This is exactly how our Savior was treated, and this is exactly what he said our lot would be. We should never expect a fair shake or whine when it is not given. We are not to play the victim. That is disloyalty to Christ. Os Guinness writes: "Followers of Christ flinch at times from the pain of wounds and the smart of slights, but that cost is in the contract of the way of the cross.... No child of a sovereign God whom we can call our Father is ever a victim or in a minority."[3]

This is why Jesus finished his comments with, "Therefore do not fear them, for there is nothing covered that will not be revealed, and hidden that will not be known" (Matthew 10:26). Listen carefully to those words: *Do not fear them.* Jesus is with us. And he promises a final day of reckoning. As someone put it, "There is a justice, and one day they shall feel it."

But even this ultimate victory should not be our immediate concern. If you want to know how I fight off discouragement, consider these words of Alan Keyes that I have posted in my study: "It is not for us to calculate our victory or fear our defeat, but to do our duty and leave the rest in God's hands."

As ambassadors, we measure our legitimacy by faithfulness and obedience to Christ, who alone will bring the increase. The most important gauge of our success will not be our numbers or even our impact, but our fidelity to our Savior.

That opportunity for faithfulness might be a salesman at the front door, a chance encounter at the bank, a casual conversation on an airplane, or chatting with a waitress in a restaurant. It could be anyplace, anytime. If you apply the right tactics, with God's help a lost and confused person will not only see the problem — his own rebellion — but also the solution — Jesus Christ. The question you need to answer in advance is, "When God opens that door, will I be ready?"

Study these tactics and learn how they work. They will serve you well when you need them. Know the truth. Know your Bible well enough to give an accurate answer. Tactics are not a substitute for knowledge. Cleverness without truth is manipulation.

Push yourself beyond your comfort zone. Begin to mix it up with others *before* you feel adequately prepared. You'll learn best by immediately putting your tactics into play, even though you may falter a bit at first. That is part of the learning process. Along the way, you'll discover what the other side has to offer, which often is not very much.

Do not be discouraged by outward appearances. Don't get caught in the trap of trying to assess the effectiveness of your conversations by their immediate, visible results. Even though a person rejects what you say, you may have put a stone in his shoe nonetheless. These things often take time. The harvest is often a season away.

Finally, live out the virtues of a good ambassador. Represent Christ in a winsome and attractive way. You — God's own representative — are the key to making a difference for the kingdom. Show the world that Christianity is worth thinking about.

With God's help, go out and give 'em Heaven.

THE AMBASSADOR'S CREED

An ambassador is ...

- Ready. An ambassador is alert for chances to represent Christ and will not back away from a challenge or an opportunity.
- Patient. An ambassador won't quarrel, but will listen in order to understand, then with gentleness will seek to respectfully engage those who disagree.
- Reasonable. An ambassador has informed convictions (not just feelings), gives reasons, asks questions, aggressively seeks answers, and will not be stumped by the same challenge twice.
- Tactical. An ambassador adapts to each unique person and situation, maneuvering with wisdom to challenge bad thinking, presenting the truth in an understandable and compelling way.

- Clear. An ambassador is careful with language and will not rely on Christian lingo nor gain unfair advantage by resorting to empty rhetoric.
- Fair. An ambassador is sympathetic and understanding toward others and will acknowledge the merits of contrary views.
- Honest. An ambassador is careful with the facts and will not misrepresent another's view, overstate his own case, or understate the demands of the gospel.
- Humble. An ambassador is provisional in his claims, knowing that his understanding of truth is fallible. He will not press a point beyond what his evidence allows.
- Attractive. An ambassador will act with grace, kindness, and good manners. He will not dishonor Christ in his conduct.
- Dependent. An ambassador knows that effectiveness requires joining his best efforts with God's power.

NOTES

CHAPTER 1: DIPLOMACY OR D-DAY?

1. Note, for example, Paul's comments in Ephesians 6:10 – 20.
2. Sometimes offensive and defensive apologetics are called positive and negative apologetics, respectively.
3. Hugh Hewitt, *In, But Not Of* (Nashville: Thomas Nelson, 2003), 166.
4. If you follow our radio program, either live or on the web (www.str.org), you'll notice I take pains not to abuse callers who disagree with me.

CHAPTER 2: RESERVATIONS

1. See 2 Timothy 2:24 – 25.
2. E.g., Acts 18:4, Acts 26:28, Acts 28:24, 2 Corinthians 5:11.
3. 1 John 4:8.
4. Isaiah 1:18.
5. 1 Corinthians 3:6 – 8.
6. I am thankful to Kathy Englert who first introduced me to this concept many years ago.

CHAPTER 3: GETTING IN THE DRIVER'S SEAT: THE COLUMBO TACTIC

1. Hugh Hewitt, *In, But Not Of* (Nashville, TN: Thomas Nelson, 2003), 172 – 73.
2. Ibid., 173; emphasis added.
3. See also Matthew 17:25, 18:12, 21:28 – 32; Mark 12:35 – 37; Luke 7:40 – 42, 14:1 – 6, 10:25 – 37; and John 18:22 – 23.
4. I'm grateful to Kevin Bywater of Summit Ministries for the improvements he helped make on the questions used in Columbo.
5. The Stand to Reason booklet, *Jesus the Only Way*, contains one hundred verses proving this point. They are taken from the teaching of Jesus and those he trained as followers. For the sake of argument, Jesus and his followers might have been mistaken about his claim to exclusivity, but make no mistake about what claim they were actually making. The booklet is available at www.str.org.

6. I believe in such arguments and even offer them (e.g., "Has God Spoken?"), but I don't think this is the most effective way to persuade on this issue.

CHAPTER 4: COLUMBO STEP TWO: THE BURDEN OF PROOF

1. I first heard this quip from apologist Phil Fernandes.
2. When neighborhood evangelists knock on your door, you might also ask, "Why should I trust that your organization — e.g., the Mormon Church, the Watchtower, etc. — speaks for God?"
3. Richard Dawkins, *The Blind Watchmaker* (London: W.W. Norton, 1996), 89.
4. Philosopher Richard Swinburne calls this the "principle of credulity," a notion accepted by most philosophers and by all ordinary folk.

CHAPTER 5: STEP THREE: USING COLUMBO TO LEAD THE WAY

1. Incidentally, I rarely use Columbo in an on-air, crossfire environment because the clock is always ticking. The more time the other person is given, the less opportunity I have to make my points. I do not want to surrender valuable airtime to my opponent by asking questions he may take a long time answering. It is difficult to get the floor back once I've given it away. The exception to this rule is when *I* am the host. In that case, I am "the man with the microphone" and can keep the conversation from becoming too one-sided.
2. This phrase was suggested to me by Frank Beckwith.
3. They might attempt to sidestep this challenge by saying, "I think my views are right *for me*. You're trying to force your views on others; I'm not." I call this the "postmodern two-step" because I think it is intellectually dishonest. The whole reason the other person is engaging you is to correct you. He thinks you should adopt his more "tolerant" view instead of the "arrogant" and "intolerant" view you hold. He wants to change your mind because he thinks his view is correct and yours is wrong, the very same thing that brings his charge of intolerance against you.
4. These are classically known as *ad hominem* attacks, literally "to the person." They are attempts to distract from the main issue by attacking the messenger in some way instead of addressing the message.

5. Jonathan Wells, *Icons of Evolution — Science or Myth?* (Washington, DC: Regnery, 2000), 79–80.

6. The professor has made what is known as a *category error*. This mistake is made when trying to assign a certain quality or action to something that does not properly belong to that category of things. If I were to ask, "How much do your thoughts weigh?" or "What does the color yellow sound like?" I would be guilty of this error.

7. The term *a priori* refers to that which is known before, or "prior to," a process of discovery, in particular, discovery by sense experience. It is often used to describe philosophical commitments that are brought to the table as defining elements of a debate before other relevant evidence is considered. These commitments determine how the evidence will be viewed or whether it will be considered at all. *A priori* is contrasted to *a posteriori,* that which is known *after* looking at the evidence of sense experience. The deliverances of science can properly be based only on *a posteriori* evidence, not on *a priori* assumptions.

8. The phrase *non sequitur* literally means "it does not follow." It describes a reply that has no relevance to what preceded it, a conclusion that does not follow from any earlier statements or evidence. To claim that the Gospels are unreliable because they were written by Christians is a non sequitur. It does not follow that simply because the Gospel writers were disciples of Christ they distorted their descriptions of him. In fact, just the opposite might be argued. Those who were closest to Jesus were in the best position to give an accurate record of the details of his life. This is not a non sequitur, but a reasonable conclusion.

9. C. S. Lewis opens with this argument in *Mere Christianity,* his fine introduction to the Christian faith. I develop this idea in more detail in chapter 6.

10. Of course, I'm not suggesting we never take a strong stand, only that as a tactical consideration, we present our views in a way that keeps our options open. Since our own understanding of truth is fallible, it is wise not to press our point beyond what our evidence allows. This is appropriate epistemic humility.

CHAPTER 6: PERFECTING COLUMBO

1. I call this approach to abortion "Only One Question" because answering a single question about abortion is the key to cutting the Gordian knot on this controversial issue. Here is that question: What is the

unborn? As I have argued elsewhere (e.g., in *Precious Unborn Human Persons*), if the unborn is not a human being, no justification for abortion is necessary. However, if the unborn is a human being, no justification for elective abortion is adequate, because we do not take the lives of valuable human beings for the reasons people give to justify their abortions. My theoretical question to the actor's wife trades on that strategy.

CHAPTER 7: SUICIDE: VIEWS THAT SELF-DESTRUCT

1. I heard this line from my friend, philosopher David Horner.
2. More precisely, "A" cannot be "non-A" at the same time, in the same way or, in Aristotle's words, "One cannot say of something that it is and that it is not in the same respect and at the same time."
3. This quip came from my clever friend Frank Beckwith.
4. These last three are memorable malaprops of Yogi Berra.
5. The argument fails, though, as many have shown. There is no inherent contradiction between God's goodness and power and the existence of evil.
6. This is not a meaningful limitation on the Divine, however. God's omnipotence ensures that he can do anything power is capable of doing. Yet no amount of power can make a square circle. It would be a limit, though, if God's rational nature were compromised by contradiction.
7. According to postmodern thinking, truth does not exist in the sense most of us use the word. There are no claims about the way the world really is that we can know to be accurate. Instead, there are many socially constructed accounts of reality, and each one is literally "true" for those who believe it.
8. C. S. Lewis, *God in the Dock* (Grand Rapids: Eerdmans, 1970), 272.
9. Empiricism, the claim that knowledge is restricted to that which can be perceived by the senses, self-destructs in the same way. The truth of empiricism itself cannot be perceived with the senses.

CHAPTER 8: PRACTICAL SUICIDE

1. For the full transcript, see "A Conversation with Lee" at www.str.org. It's a delightful lesson in the use of the Suicide Tactic.
2. Alvin Plantinga, "Pluralism," in *The Philosophical Challenge of Religious Diversity,* ed. Philip Quinn and Kevin Meeker (New York: Oxford University Press, 2000), 177.
3. C. S. Lewis, *Mere Christianity* (New York: Macmillan, 1952), 5.

4. Gregory Koukl and Francis Beckwith, *Relativism — Feet Firmly Planted in Mid-Air* (Grand Rapids: Baker, 1998), 143.
5. Jeffery L. Sheler, "Unwelcome Prayers," *U.S. News & World Report,* 20 September 1999.

CHAPTER 9: SIBLING RIVALRY AND INFANTICIDE

1. Incidentally, in the Christian view the conflict is resolved because God's love is not sentimental, but sacrificial. He can execute justice while also making provision for mercy and forgiveness.
2. C. S. Lewis, *Mere Christianity* (New York: Macmillan, 1952), 31.
3. G. K. Chesterton, *Orthodoxy* (Garden City, NY: Doubleday, 1959), 41, as quoted in Ravi Zacharias, *Deliver Us from Evil* (Dallas: Word Publishing, 1996), 95 – 96.
4. I don't think this is a sound way of reasoning because it commits the is/ought fallacy. I am only adopting this claim for the sake of argument (see chapter 10, "Taking the Roof Off").
5. Lewis, *Mere Christianity,* 31.
6. Richard Taylor, *Ethics, Faith, and Reason* (Englewood Cliffs, NJ: Prentice-Hall, 1985), 83 – 84.
7. *The Quarrel,* directed by Eli Cohen, distributed by Honey and Apple Film Corporation, Canada, 1991.
8. This problem could also be stated as a Sibling Rivalry: (1) God does not exist as moral lawmaker. Therefore, there are no moral laws to break. Therefore, evil does not exist. (2) Evil exists. Therefore, transcendent moral laws exist. Therefore, a transcendent moral lawmaker exists. Therefore, God exists. Either there is no God and no evil, or evil exists and so does God. The option that does not seem possible is that evil exists, but God does not. These notions are in conflict, victims of Sibling Rivalry.
9. If the atheist does not affirm the existence of objective evil, but is merely pointing out what appears to be a contradiction in the theist's worldview, he escapes this particular dilemma. Usually, however, the atheist raising this objection actually believes in genuine evil.
10. J. P. Moreland, *Christianity and the Nature of Science* (Grand Rapids: Baker, 1989), 104.

CHAPTER 10: TAKING THE ROOF OFF

1. Francis Schaeffer, *The God Who Is There,* in *The Complete Works of Francis Schaeffer* (Wheaton, IL: Crossway Books, 1982), 1:138.

2. Ibid., 140 – 141.

3. Ibid., 110.

4. Romans 13:3 – 4, 1 Peter 2:14.

5. This tale is almost certainly an urban legend. I include it for two reasons. First, even if apocryphal, it still illustrates this tactic well. Second, this story has circulated so widely that you might encounter this "proof" of atheism and need a response.

6. I owe this insight to Scott Klusendorf.

7. This was the very approach I took with the witch from Wisconsin in chapter 1. It is possible that the person would counter that a fetus is not a human being in the same sense that a one-year-old is. My response is, "I suppose you could also say that a fourteen-year-old is not a human being in the same sense that a one-year-old is — as in growth and maturity — but that person is still a human being in every way."

CHAPTER 11: STEAMROLLER

1. You might be wondering how being in the hot seat (mentioned in chapter 4) is different from getting steamrolled. In the former, you are merely *overmatched*. With steamrollers, you are *overwhelmed*. You may be up to the task of answering the objection, but you are never really given the opportunity.

2. William Dembski, ed., *Darwin's Nemesis* (Downers Grove, IL: InterVarsity Press, 2006), 102.

CHAPTER 12: RHODES SCHOLAR

1. Norman Geisler and Ronald Brooks, *Come Let us Reason Together* (Grand Rapids: Baker, 1996), 99.

2. Douglas Geivett, "A Particularist View," in *Four Views on Salvation in a Pluralistic World*, ed. Dennis Okholm and Timothy Phillips (Grand Rapids: Zondervan, 1996), 266 – 67.

3. Douglas Futuyma, *Science on Trial: The Case for Evolution* (Sunderland, MA: Sinauer Associates, Inc., 1983), 12; emphasis added.

4. Richard Lewontin, "Billions and Billions of Demons," *New York Review of Books*, January 4, 1997; emphasis in the original.

5. Robert Funk, Roy Hoover, and the Jesus Seminar, *The Five Gospels: What Did Jesus Really Say?* (New York: Macmillan, 1993), 5; quoted in J. P. Moreland and Michael Wilkins, *Jesus Under Fire* (Grand Rapids: Zondervan, 1995), 4; emphasis added.

6. I owe this insight to J. P. Moreland.

CHAPTER 13: JUST THE FACTS, MA'AM

1. Dennis Prager, *Ultimate Issues,* July – September, 1989.
2. Donald McFarlan, ed., *Guinness Book of World Records 1992* (New York: Facts on File, Inc., 1991), 92.
3. John Eidsmoe, *Christianity and the Constitution* (Grand Rapids: Baker, 1987), 43.
4. Find a detailed response in "The Da Vinci Code Cracks" at www.str.org.
5. Dan Brown, *The Da Vinci Code* (New York: Doubleday, 2003), 231 – 34.
6. Philip Schaff, *History of the Christian Church,* Vol. III (Grand Rapids: Eerdmans, 1994), 623, 629.
7. Brown, *The Da Vinci Code,* 125.
8. Find a video clip of this conversation at http://www.leestrobel.com/videoserver/video.php?clip=strobelT1123.
9. Matthew 18:15 – 20, Galatians 6:1.
10. John 3:17; 12:47; 5:22, 27; Acts 10:42; 17:31.

CHAPTER 14: MORE SWEAT, LESS BLOOD

1. Charles Colson, *Kingdoms in Conflict* (Zondervan: 1987), 255.
2. An irrefutable biblical argument for the deity of Christ based on John 1:3 is featured in the article "The Deity of Christ: Case Closed," found at www.str.org.
3. Os Guinness and John Seel, *No God But God* (Chicago: Moody Press, 1992), 91.